LETTERS FROM A LANCASTER GUNNER

LETTERS FROM A LANCASTER GUNNER

HELEN THOMPSON

FONTHILL

Fonthill Media Language Policy

Fonthill Media publishes in the international English language market. One language edition is published worldwide. As there are minor differences in spelling and presentation, especially with regard to American English and British English, a policy is necessary to define which form of English to use. The Fonthill Policy is to use the form of English native to the author. Helen Thompson was born and educated in Birmingham, UK; therefore British English has been adopted in this publication.

Fonthill Media Limited
Fonthill Media LLC
www.fonthillmedia.com
office@fonthillmedia.com

First published in the United Kingdom and the United States of America 2019

British Library Cataloguing in Publication Data:
A catalogue record for this book is available from the British Library

ISBN 978-1-78155-698-6

Typeset in 10.5pt on 13pt MinionPro
Printed and bound in England

For my dad, Brian, and Aunty Joyce.
My labour of love, to do justice to your brother and hero, Joe.

The pain has stopped, for I am dead,
My time on earth is done.
But in a hundred years from now
I'll still be twenty-one.

My brief, sweet life is over
My eyes no longer see,
No summer walks, no Christmas trees,
No pretty girls for me.

I've got the chop, I've had it.
My nightly ops are done.
Yet in another hundred years
I'll still be twenty-one.

'Requiem for an Air Gunner'
R. W. Gilbert

Prologue

The following pages will attempt to do justice to the story of Flight Sergeant Joseph Henry Thompson, otherwise known as 'Mac'.

Joseph, or Joe to the family and Mac to his mates, was my uncle; the oldest brother and hero of my father, Brian, but we never actually met. As a child, I can remember that a photograph of Joe held a subdued but permanent place in a frame on top of my Nan Olive's old china cabinet in the corner of her little sitting room. I can recall being curious about the man in the picture. He was not a person who was familiar to me, not a presence in my life, and I was inquisitive about why his image warranted such a prominent position among the small and rather exclusive display of trinkets. I remember that there was an overwhelming sense of taboo about this subject, and when I did venture an enquiry, I was left with a lasting feeling that I had asked the wrong question at the wrong time, and that I should probably not do so again.

Regrettably, I did exactly that. No more questions were asked, at least until I was in my mid-forties and, like Olive, a mother of four children of my own. At the time, I was looking into our family history: collating the Thompson family tree and researching the characters and stories within it. Over a cup of tea with my father and his older sister, my Aunt Joyce, one day I happened to enquire, tentatively, about their oldest brother, Joe. I was eager to learn more about this mysterious young man who had throughout my childhood been a constant presence by way of that discreet, faded photograph at my nan's house, while simultaneously being entirely physically absent for the first forty-three years of my life.

The conversation was both surprising and inspiring. I was riveted by the story of their brother, the hero. When my aunt declared somewhat nonchalantly that she thought there might be 'some very old wartime letters which Joe and mom wrote to each other in a box' in her spare bedroom, my heart almost left my chest. It was incredible to think that something so precious could be hidden away unacknowledged, although my aunt seemed equally as surprised by my interest as I was by her revelation. She had not intentionally kept them secret of course, but clearly the years had rushed by while life had taken a front seat, and my aunt's natural instinct to bury difficult memories deeply and forever had taken precedent as time had progressed. So here we now were, sixty-three years after the letters had been written, the stars had finally aligned, and the stories were transferring to a new generation of the Thompson dynasty.

Both my father and I became voracious in our desire to lap up the contents of the letters. My dad took them home first and read them lovingly, placing them neatly in chronological order, then transcribing each one into a notebook. He diligently appended each page with dates, notes, and thoughts. He connected the dots and posed questions. In short, he remembered his brother afresh. His recollections of Joe up to this point had been a fantasy, a child's view of the life and adventures of his grown-up brother in air force blue.

Our shared passion for Joe's story endured as we conducted the enormous amounts of research required to complete the puzzle, long before deciding to attempt to put Joe's story into a book. Together we applied for Joe's RAF service records, hospital files, and his Bomber Command clasp. I played detective, researching the air bases where Joe was stationed during the war, and wrote countless letters to Squadron Associations, historians, and the Goldfish Club. I posted on online forums, scoured ancient newspaper clippings and family history websites, buried myself in the National Archives at Kew, and sent for birth, marriage, and death certificates, the results of which were all relayed to my dad and aunt in detail.

The letters cover the period from December 1943 when Joe signed up at eighteen years of age, up to September 1947 when, at the age of twenty-two, Joe's writings suddenly cease, for reasons which I will allow the reader to discover in their natural order. They are a journal of the fascinating, funny, terrifying, extraordinary, and ordinary things that happened over that four-year period of life in wartime RAF. During this time, Joe describes his training as a mid-upper gunner; we get to know his mates and fellow crew members; there are boyish pranks and (lots of) letters from girls; he takes us on active operations over Nazi Germany; he is shot down into the North Sea; and he falls in love with a girl from Liverpool.

Correspondence, of course, is rarely a one-sided exercise, and Olive wrote back regularly with news from home. Her letters are filled with love, advice, and provide fascinating insight into the perspective of a widow trying to keep calm and carry on with no husband, little money, and four young children. The gaps have been filled by the memories of my aunt and others, whose assistance in this regard has been invaluable.

I have taken the decision to populate the pages of this book with some of Joe's original words in the form of his handwritten letters, and by the inclusion of the few surviving family photographs which remain. That is, after all, the point of the exercise and was the catalyst for this entire process. I hope to lay out this story truthfully, warts and all, since my family were then, and remain still, ordinary Birmingham folk, with flaws and emotions, rather than fictional heroes and heroines. My words will only add context to the detailed story that Joe has left for us so beautifully in his own words.

The story you will read is true to Joe's version of events and representative of both his and Olive's views and characters, so any historical inaccuracies are unintentional.

This book is my attempt to lay down for posterity the story of the young man who was never talked about, so that the future generations of my family, and others, may understand why he was, and shall always remain, our hero.

CONTENTS

1

Growing Up Fast

The Thompsons
Birmingham, 1925–1943

It was a cold December morning when Joe left home to begin the journey that would take, quite literally, the rest of his life.

Born Joseph Henry Thompson on 26 June 1925, Joe was the first-born child of Olive and her newly-wed husband, Joseph, from whom the baby took his name. The house in to which he made his entrance to the world was No. 1 Frederick Street, in the Sparkhill area of the sprawling industrial city of Birmingham. It was an uninspiring neighbourhood at best, unpleasant at worst, and it was a place from which his mother was desperate to escape.

The young Joe shared more with his father than just a name. He had dark, chocolate brown eyes and thick, tight-curled hair, which would grow in to an unruly, wiry textured mop as he turned from boy to man. His father was a tall man, and Joe, along with the two brothers and sister who were yet to join him, would also turn out to be a 6-footer with a slim, athletic build.

Unlike his son, however, who was mild and cheeky of temperament, Joseph Snr was a strict Victorian parent. His life had been tough and filled with hard, physical labour, working as an aluminium moulder in Birmingham's prominent gun-making industry. He spent long days casting fitments for weapons in one of the small workshops, which had grown up in the former backyards of the labyrinth of houses in the area of the city that had become known to locals as the 'Gun Quarter'. Numerous workshops existed, each specialising in the production of one specific part of a gun, with up to fifty workshops combining in a conveyor-belt style approach to weapon construction. The long hours and cramped conditions were bad enough, but the additional hazard of metal dust and the other unhealthy by-products of the manufacturing processes exacerbated the difficulty of working in such an environment.

At thirty-four years old, and eight years Olive's senior, Joseph Snr's poor wages were still only just enough to furnish his tiny, but growing family with lodgings in 'rooms' in Sparkhill, south of the city centre. His journey to work from here was either a one-hour each way walk, or a long tram ride, and Olive hated living there. The arrival of this, her first son, had ignited a fire within her that made her yearn for a better, more salubrious 'nest' in which to relocate her family.

Both Olive and Joseph Snr's families had originated from rural areas outside of the city, but it was Joseph Snr's father (another Joseph) who, seeking a profession as a Police Constable, had brought them within the city boundaries. Eventually both had settled their respective families in the Aston area, which is where Olive and Joseph were simultaneously residing when they married.

At the time of little Joe's birth, Olive was twenty-six years old. She had heard talk about the programmes of new-build Council Housing on the outskirts of Birmingham, which she now dreamed could create a fresh start for her family, as well as serving up a bonus in the form of distance between Olive and her in-laws, of whom she was neither fond nor approving.

A moral individual, Olive fully intended to raise Joe to be the same. And so, she did. For the first five years of Joe's life, he remained the only son. Olive put all her efforts in to the care of her husband and son, passing on her sense of respectability and teaching Joe the rights and wrongs of being a caring and thoughtful human being.

Brother Dennis arrived as Joe began school. It was during Olive's confinement at the Sorrento Nursing Home (a Council-owned premises designed to assist women on low income with childbirth) that Olive's dream of a new home became a reality. Her husband collected the keys to their new two-bedroomed semi-detached council home in Northfield. Olive, Joseph, and their two little boys moved into 16 Elmdale Grove shortly afterwards, and it would remain Olive's home until her final days.

Dennis was followed two years later in 1931 by his only sister, Joyce, and the youngest of Joe's three siblings, my own father, Brian, was born in October 1934, when Joe was nine years old.

Joe attended school at Tinker's Farm, a brand-new school that was set up in temporary buildings in order to accommodate the influx of families who had moved in to the new Council Housing estates, which were rapidly expanding during the interwar years.

He neither excelled nor failed as a student. School uniform was a second-hand suit jacket and cut off, baggy shorts, as that was all that his parents could afford. He received a reasonable education at Tinker's Farm, becoming an articulate boy who was a little 'rough around the edges'. His sense of fun was infectious, but he was a thoughtful and handsome boy with a glorious smile.

Life was tough but felt strangely idyllic for the Thompson siblings. Outside of school, days were filled with street games, cricket, marbles, tip-cat, and hide and seek, and the new house, placed conveniently at the top of a cul-de-sac of homes, provided plenty of other scruffy kids to play with when your resident sibling playmates became too dull.

As a young teenager, Joe took his first part-time job as a delivery boy to Mr Bourne, the local grocer, and he became a popular figure with the local customers.

Everything changed one Sunday in September 1939 when a morning radio broadcast by Chamberlain announced that Britain was at war with Germany. This was a moment that my father always recollected for his entire life, although at the time he had failed to grasp its significance. It was a bringer of major changes for Joe, who, at the age of fourteen, left school and took his first full-time job at the Austin Motor Company.

Affectionately known as 'The Austin', it employed somewhere near 30,000 local people during the war years in its huge manufacturing plant at Longbridge, close to the Thompson family home. The factory, a giant automobile producer during peacetime, now became a critical manufacturing plant for both motor vehicles for the British Armed Forces, as well as producing a formidable list of parts such as fuel tanks, Rolls-Royce engine parts, and wing sections for aircraft. In the days leading up to the start of the war, 120 acres of factory were magically 'disappeared' into the countryside by a huge camouflaging exercise, ensuring its relative safety, if not immunity, from attack by enemy aircraft throughout the duration of the Second World War.

Joseph's job was as a wood machinist's mate, learning and assisting the skilled machinists in their production activities. At this time, the vast majority of The Austin's workers were women, and although Joe could not have predicted it, his mother would soon be joining their ranks as an employee, as life was about to take another unexpected turn.

Early on the morning of 22 April 1941, a Tuesday, Olive awoke to discover her husband dead beside her. He had been suffering, like many others who had worked in the Victorian industrial cities of the late nineteenth and early twentieth centuries, from bronchitis. His health had been further exacerbated by the conditions within which he worked, with constant dust plaguing his lungs. A post-mortem revealed that Joseph Snr had been coping with emphysema, and a bout of pneumonia had finally invaded his already war-torn lungs to contribute to his demise at the age of fifty-one. Joe Jnr was just short of his sixteenth birthday as he was suddenly thrust in to a new role as the man of the house.

Joyce's memory of this time is clear—a morning off school on the day her father died, then being packed back off to class in the afternoon with six-year-old Brian attached to one hand and an explanatory note about their brief absence in the other. A typically stoic Olive had either concluded that the show must go on or that she would be better able to manage herself and her grief that afternoon without the additional burden of having children present as witnesses. Perhaps a little of both.

Few memories of their father survived for Joyce or Brian into their adulthood, save for his strictness and the enormous treat of the gift of a whole Mars Bar on Joyce's third birthday. So much would happen from this point on in all their lives that the loss of the head of the family would seem a distant and foggy memory, but one thing was for sure, it would fortify Olive in a way she could never have imagined, enabling her to cope with the challenges lying ahead.

The war was in full swing at the time of this sudden and devastating tragedy for the Thompsons, but the hardships which the conflict had already brought were nothing in comparison to the difficulties that now lay ahead for the widowed Olive and her four children.

Joe was now forced to work as many hours as possible in order to sustain their independent existence. The relationship between the grieving Olive and her eldest son grew closer as the months passed. Her reliance upon him for support both emotionally and financially pushed the adolescent Joe in to a level of maturity far beyond his years. Where other boys were forging social lives and going out in the evenings, Joe piled his wages into the family pot and stayed home to help Olive when and where he could.

The war's progress quickly became a topic of great interest for the whole family, but especially for Joe, who was constantly switching on the wireless to hear the news or checking the *Daily Express* for the latest from the battle fronts.

The RAF held a particular fascination for Joe, and at sixteen years old, he joined a squadron of the newly formed ATC (Air Training Corps) in order to extend his knowledge and prepare himself for potential future combat. He excelled. Reading manuals on aircraft recognition and becoming adept at this in practice by watching the noisy planes which had been flying over his Birmingham home since the war began. He studied whatever he could get his hands on in the way of military books and magazines and he had one eye firmly fixed on joining up when he turned eighteen.

The ATC was growing at a spectacular rate at this time, and Joe knew that it would be by far the best way to enter the RAF when the time came.

Joe was growing up fast and he had grown in to a good-looking boy with a mop of thick black hair. He neither encouraged nor discouraged his accidental tendency to be a bit of a girl-magnet, and was a diligent and thoughtful boy to his mother. He punctuated his hard work with customary good humour and teasing his little sister was fast becoming his favourite pastime. He had few regrets about leaving his school days behind and helping his mother with the younger kids.

He had committed to Olive, however, that, unlike so many of his peers at the time, he would resist the urge to lie about his age in a bid to enter the war early. As a widow with a house full of kids, he knew that he needed to balance Olive's need for family income carefully with her need for his presence, so he would wait until he turned eighteen before taking any steps toward joining up.

That day came soon enough. Joe celebrated his eighteenth birthday in June 1943. Just four weeks thereafter, on 26 July, Joe enlisted. A tram journey to Viceroy Close in Edgbaston to 21 ACSB (Air Crew Selection Board) was all that was required, where he undertook selection tests and exams in maths and English, as well as medical tests, and assessments for fitness and colour blindness, among others.

The SMA3 test (Sensory Motor Apparatus) was a screening that examined the dexterity of potential aircrew, bearing in mind their requirement to be able to operate a turret or to work a trigger with appropriate reaction times. In addition to this, the RAF were in the habit of including questions relating to the candidates' interests. Particular attention was paid to regional accents and the kind of clubs the men belonged to, in order to ascertain their social standing, which seemed to hold more sway for selection here than in any of the other services at the time. Joe, in spite of his working-class roots and Brummy accent, was accepted for training, and four days later, with a Grade 1 medical categorisation under his belt asserting him to be fit for full flying duties, he was recommended for training as an air gunner. He had now only to wait for a vacancy at one of the Receiving Centres when he would be called to join the ranks of the other RAF recruits.

The air gunnery route was not necessarily the career path that he had hoped for, but Joe was happy that it would get him flying anyway. Like so many other young men, Joe considered Bomber Command as a 'safe bet'. There was something about the idea of being in the air that both fascinated him and made him feel as though his route through the remainder of the war would be less hazardous than a spell in the army. Plus, he knew he would look good in blue.

2

Bedding In

Joe
Air Crew Receiving Centre, Regent's Park, London
31 December 1943–15 January 1944

Joe had spent a short Christmas with Olive, the children, and a selection of Olive's many siblings and their families at Elmdale Grove before the call to service finally came. The Christmas break had been joyful but bittersweet; knowing that it may be his last at home for some time, both he and Olive were feeling emotional as the days ticked by.

After a stoic farewell to his mother and the kids, Joe also said goodbye to 1943 and his boyhood when he took the train from Birmingham New Street to London Euston. His destination was No. 1 Air Crew Receiving Centre (ACRC), on Avenue Road in Regent's Park, but the designated muster point was the Lord's cricket ground close by. He arrived there safely at 3 p.m. and presented himself for duty. The letter he had received had told him to bring the 'minimum of personal requirements', so his small suitcase was no burden on the long journey. Hundreds of men per week were being inducted through the centre, and they were subsequently split into groups of around fifty to sixty, each of which made up a 'Flight'. Joe was assigned to 6 Flight, 131 Intake, and officially adopted his new moniker of 3050664 Thompson.

Joe was billeted with ten other young men, all in the same room, in what he described as a 'posh' flat in Maida Vale, one of the many large buildings that had been requisitioned in the area surrounding Regent's Park during the war. As well as accommodation, the military had taken over various other offices and buildings in the local area, including the conveniently placed London Zoo, which handed over part of its facilities to serve as a canteen for the recruits from the ACRC.

They were told that they would remain at Regent's Park for approximately nineteen days, during which time they would undertake basic training, learn about RAF discipline and procedures, and be rigorously tested for various skills and medical issues. A posting would then follow to a place that would take each recruit on to the next, more specialised phase of their training.

Joe soon discovered that his sense of humour and naturally mischievous character would stand him in very good stead here. The ACRC was a hot-bed of youth and along with youth came a certain inevitable level of hijinks and prank-playing that young men employ in order to pass the slower hours. As one of four children, Joe was well accustomed to rough and tumble and teasing behaviour, and he put his skills to good use at the ACRC.

One evening, true to form, he and two of his roommates prepared what they considered to be a rather ingenious surprise for the remainder of the chaps in their billet. Nothing if not innovative, they had taken the time and care to sew up the blankets on their beds, into which they had poured their webbing and mess-tins to ensure 'maximum comfort' at bed time. If this rather time-consuming caper had not been enough, the master-stroke that concluded the prank had been their work to diligently remove a number of springs from the beds beneath. The prank was every bit worth the effort and there was not a dry eye in the house by the time it was over.

No doubt this was neither the first nor last such enterprise among Joe's chums over the period of their captivity at the ACRC or beyond. Tomfoolery was an unspoken form of camaraderie among the young men away from home for the first time, and an inevitable outcome of the juxtaposition of youth with warfare.

Joe got wind quite early on of the rumoured location for his next move, although it was a place he had never even heard of, somewhere on the north-east coast by the sea. It was an indication of the youth, naïveté, and inexperience of Joe that the existence of the mysterious 'Whitley Bay' came as a revelation to him, and he knew only roughly where it was located and that it had been named as one of his potential destinations. Time would tell.

Joe's wages were a much-needed boost to the family's income, and as Joe had grown older and the war showed little sign of abating, he knew that he would be required to send the money home to Olive. Used to a weekly wage, it came as a bit of an unpleasant shock to Joe to discover that the RAF paid fortnightly, but he set about dutifully arranging for a voluntary deduction from his salary to be sent to his mother. There was a minimum requirement for Joe to pay his mother an allowance of 6*d* per day, but Joe requested this deduction to be increase to 1*s* and 6*d*, which was half of his daily pay. Olive's thoughtful son was, without his mother's encouragement, taking his responsibility as the man of the house seriously and he began collecting his pay at the fortnightly pay parade with pride and satisfaction.

The first few days were all about the issue of extensive kit, regulation ninety-second clipper haircuts, getting to know the 'routine', and, of course, vaccinations. These were given to protect the men against diphtheria, typhoid, and smallpox. There was always a long queue for injections, which were given in both arms and almost invariably someone in the queue would faint while waiting for their turn. Needles were used repeatedly, of course, until blunt enough to draw blood in their unlucky final victims. Health and safety regulations were not so advanced as to recognise the potential risks of disease transmission as a result of attempted disease prevention, and Joe could look forward to the prospect of some of these inoculations (and the subsequent sore arms that accompanied them) at regular three-month intervals for the rest of his RAF career.

The first extensive time away from home for Joe and many of the other teens, it was something of an adventure, which felt like a grown-up version of the Youth Camps that many of them had enjoyed during summer breaks from school. Nicknames were allocated liberally to both people and places, whether wanted or not, and the Receiving Centre became affectionately known as the 'Aysee Arsey'.

For the somewhat sheltered young lad from suburban Birmingham, the Regent's Park ACRC was a bit of an eye-opener. It was awash with all nationalities—Indian, French, Honduran, Canadian, New Zealanders. There were sailors, airmen, and all pick of infantry rubbing shoulders with each other, and as a result, a recurring problem with theft, of which the RAF was well aware.

Joe's first indication of the presence of a more light-fingered contingent among his fellow trainees came on only his third day. Several recruits were sent up before the Commanding Officer for losing parts of their kit. Orders were given that they would have to fork out personally to pay for replacements, and each was put on a charge as punishment for their carelessness. This ignited a vigilance in Joe who was well aware that the value of a full kit was in excess of £20, or at least that was the official RAF mantra that had been spun.

Despite his care and attention, only a few days later, Joe's shaving brush and mug were stolen from a padlocked kit bag. It cost a pretty penny to replace them from the stores and as he reluctantly parted with the 10*s* 9*d* it cost to buy new ones, he was not sure whether he felt more livid about the money or about the five hours of cookhouse fatigues that he had also received for the crime of losing his kit. He was not happy with this perceived injustice, but knew that protestations of innocence would have been futile, so Joe deferred to the only reliable course of action and went about his business to the best of his ability.

In addition to this set-back, the mundane reality of military life was also becoming apparent in other ways. Joe found that he was having to spend money here, there, and everywhere—marker pens to label his clothing with his service number, a box for his shaving kit, corn plasters, and Lifebuoy 'toilet', most of which he asked Olive to buy on his behalf and send by post. Within days he was asking his mother to send him more money. This was not what he had expected.

By the end of week one, the full wrath of RAF discipline had come down to bear upon Joe and his colleagues. The entire Flight was confined to barracks due to the unacceptable messiness of one of their rooms. Lesson well and truly learned. There was no longer a mother or sister to pick up after them, and the practical application of those domestic duties, which were, rightly or wrongly, ordinarily assigned to the ladies of the home, would prove to be an interesting learning curve for Joe as time went on.

As his service continued, Joe would find that these two issues would become among the most regular problems he would encounter, and if he was not lacking in the financial department, he would most certainly be lacking clean laundry.

As it was becoming more and more apparent that this was not a holiday, the gradual introduction of long marches with full kit, gruelling parades, cleaning rotas, and rules, rules, rules confirmed it. Lectures on RAF law, administration and organisation, mathematics, weapons, and other subjects began, as well as the inevitable PT, which took place both in the park and in the swimming pool. The latter was often blighted by the incredibly sore arms from which Joe and the other men suffered as a result of the varying injections to which they were subjected. The only perk as far as he was concerned was the calibre of his teachers, and PT became bearable when he found himself being put through his paces by a famous face. Harry Mizler, former lightweight boxing champion of Great Britain, was in charge of Joe's fourth PT session, and he was instantly star struck.

His admiration extended far beyond this, however, as he became more and more cognisant of the nature and reputation of each of the instructors and officers whom he encountered. He was surprised when he noticed that some of the instructors were teaching men of higher rank than themselves, but regarded their undeniable skills with awe. There were those who guided their charges with an easy, thorough manner, and those whose war experiences spoke for themselves. All of them made an impact on Joe and inspired him to work hard and follow their lead.

There was rarely time for boredom. A particularly harsh day in January began with a two-and-a-half-hour drill, followed by a lecture, then Pay-Book Parade. A short break for dinner was quickly interrupted by a trip to Lord's cricket ground where the gas chambers tests took place. No time to rest, as the airmen were marched back to the station for one of the weekly kit inspections, which was carried out by none other than the CO. Inspection complete, Joe's sighs of relief were cut short by an immediate instruction to parade in full kit in just ten minutes. He noted how the deadly silence in the room spoke volumes, and that the tension had been further exacerbated when they gathered outside, only to be immediately dismissed on the advice that the parade was cancelled. As Joe succinctly put it, 'They've sent us all up the pole today!'

As for so many other recruits to the armed forces, the meticulous nature of daily bed inspections and weekly kit inspections confounded Joe. Every item was required to be folded in a particular way and placed in a special position, all within fifteen minutes. During this process, all shoes and boots were required to be polished, including the soles, all studs burnished and all webbing equipment taken to pieces and laid out. It was a not inconsiderable task for the men to undertake, but was one of the basic requirements that they had to learn and to accept.

In those first early days, Joe became a regular visitor to the RAF dentistry team. His first dental parade concluded with one wisdom tooth extraction and a further six teeth being earmarked for fillings. Perhaps, he realised, he ought to have paid more attention to Olive's advice on this subject as a boy. Joe's dental needs were hardly unusual, given the lack of general oral hygiene throughout the 1920s and '30s as Joe had been growing up, and as a result, only approximately 5 per cent of recruits to the military at this time were actually fully dentally fit. It was a detail that held both a sense of fascination and concurrent foreboding for Joe that the RAF dentists used dental materials that were specifically designed to reduce the likelihood of the recruits being incapacitated by the effects of high altitude. Plastic, rather than metal implants, had been proven to better deal with 'Aerodontalgia', the exceedingly painful condition that is created by the extremes of temperature and pressure caused by flying in unpressurised cabins at high altitudes. Joe knew that these experiences lay ahead of course, but he had not figured that his teeth would need to play a part in them.

It was here at the ACRC that Joe, like so many others, received his new and enduring nickname. No less than five of the eleven men in Joe's lodgings were Josephs. Each of them was cheerfully and indiscriminately allocated a pseudonym in order to help the observer with differentiation. From this point onwards, Joe became 'Mac'. Despite his efforts to find out why, he was never told the reason for the name, but it became the badge with which he would be identified thereafter among his fellow airmen, so he eventually gave up trying to find out and adopted it with the affectionate manner in which it had been given.

Mac quickly formed a bond with another of the five Josephs. He was a cheeky Liverpudlian by the name of Joe Lee and had a sense of humour that matched Mac's own. He had also been provided with a pseudonym and had submitted to becoming 'Smokey' Joe for reasons which he also never quite fathomed. Mac and Joe Lee would go on to develop the firmest of friendships as roommates, which would endure for a long time to come.

Food was turning out to be the number one problem. As a 5-foot 11½-inch eighteen-year-old boy with a large appetite, Mac was finding that the NAAFI meals were not up to the standards of his mother's home cooking. Despite all the years of low income and wretched rationing, neither Mac nor his younger siblings could ever really recall going hungry. Olive was a wizard with the meagre supplies she had and she, no doubt, regularly went without so that the children would not. The reality of RAF life was now hitting Mac firmly in the stomach.

Worse still, he soon found out that a twenty-minute break in the ill-staffed NAAFI canteen could actually take as much as ninety minutes unless you were lucky enough to evade the long queues or were friendly with the WAAFs. The servers were often rendered incapable of dishing up fast enough to service the deluge of bodies who descended upon them *en masse* and starving, and Mac suffered the consequences of these inefficiencies a number of times when he was reprimanded strongly by his corporal for being tardy on return from mealtimes. Better a reprimand than a missed dinner, however.

It was not all bad, though. A touch of glamour and excitement entered their lives on 4 January 1944 when the ACRC received a visit from the Duchess of Gloucester, Princess Alice, the Air Chief Commandant of the WAAF. There was a tone of mischief among the young men as the Duchess initiated a conversation with one of Mac's fellow airmen. For the duration of the short chat, he was seated in the dentist's chair. As the Duchess drew alongside him, she asked the young man if he liked the service, to which he apparently replied, 'Yes, Ma'am, but not his part!'

Joe was adapting well to his new life. He passed the awkward night vision test (during which the men were sat in a dark room wearing a neck restraint and asked to identify a number of objects that appeared on a screen momentarily in front of them) and swimming test with ease, he wrote a letter every day, got a lousy cold, and was told by the corporal that he looked 'slick' in air force blue.

Joe's letters home during this first period were particularly special to the family back home. His presence in their small home was greatly missed and the regular news of his new experiences was absorbed eagerly by everyone there. The children began to see Joe as a new kind of hero. His tales of Mayfair, London, cinemas, Westminster Abbey, and mealtimes at London Zoo were like scenes from a Hollywood movie. Little did Joe realise that each and every one of his letters was being placed carefully back in its envelope and filed away lovingly with the others, to be treasured and retained forever by his mother.

Mac's time at the ACRC became smoother as the days progressed and he acclimatised, coming to an end on Friday 15 January 1944. He wrote to the family about the 'secret' destination he was headed for, but shared his consternation for the manner in which they departed. A full parade at 9 p.m. was followed by over two hours standing around in heavy, back-breaking kit, until their scheduled 11.15 p.m. departure time. Contrary to the early rumours, Mac's new home would be Bridlington, rather than the predicted Whitley Bay, and there he would join 15 Initial Training Wing.

As a parting gift from the ACRC, Joe discovered that the charge against him for losing his kit had been dropped. His attention to detail with tidiness and continued good conduct had been enough to get him off the hook. The entire Flight's performance was deemed so good, in fact, that they were advised that future continued progress along the same lines would ensure that they would turn out to be one of the best that the station had ever had.

3050664 THOMPSON. ~~G~~. AC2

6. Flight. 131 Intake.

R.A.F. Station,

Avenue Close,

     "   Road,

Regent's Park

London. N.W.8.

Tues.

Dear Mom + Kids.

        I got here OK
at about 3 o'clock on Monday.
You must excuse my writing
as I've just had 2 of
those infections + may have
another tomorrow or soon
after. The ones I've had
up to now have made
us all feel groggy +
our left and right muscle

painful & stiff. Some faint
after a while. We've had
all our kit :— Tunic, Cap
"with white piece in front"—
Trousers, Great Coat. Kit-bag, all
webbing (12 pieces) mess—tin,
water Bottle, Gas cape, Gas-mask
1st aid pack, Tin Hat & Net, Shaving
Brush, Boot & Brass Brushes, "House—
wife", Knife Spoon, Fork, 1 pair
of Boots, 1 pr. shoes, 1 pr. pumps,
2 pr. Gym shorts & same Vests,
2 ordinary Vests, 2 pr. "Aertex" pants
(short kind) 1 pullover, scarf, gloves
4 prs socks, 3 Shirts, 6 collars, tie,
1 Rain Cape-cum— Ground Sheet and
lots more odds & ends. We
had to march 2 miles with
that lot at 140 paces per
minute.!! The "Grub" is a bit
rough but its all right.

We are in some very "posh" Flats at Maida Vale. There are 11 blokes in our Room and they're all pretty decent fellas. We have arranged a Rota for cleaning the room out. We Scrubbed the floor + Cleaned the windows today!! I must pause now to go on a Parade. —— To continue, We had we just had our swimming test, also a blood godding Parade Blimey my head-aches! It's those infections!! We've been told we will be here 19 days or

so + then we may
be posted to Whitny
Bay or some other place
I can't name. We've got
another infection next
week. By the way I've
just Had a vacination
with the rest. I feel
B— awful!! The
Taylor is coming tomorrow
to check out clothes.
We Parade each day
at 5·30 A.M. and get
to bed at 10.0p.m. if we're
lucky!! Must leave now
all my love
Val

3

The One-Eyed Dump

Olive
15 Initial Training Wing, Bridlington
5 Flight, 96 Intake
16 January 1944–25 February 1944

On a bright Monday morning in the middle of January, Olive took delivery of a parcel from her eldest son. The mundane nature of its contents undermined the feelings which they evoked in Olive. The parcel contained a neatly folded, paper-wrapped bundle of Joseph's 'civvy' clothes, which had finally made their way home. These were the clothes that Joe had been wearing when he had left home almost a month ago, no longer required and symbolically mailed home as a remnant of a boyhood now over. To Olive, they were the elephant in the room, signifying not only the obvious absence of her boy, but more than that: an understanding that he would most likely have no need for these items in the foreseeable future, if indeed ever.

Joe had written several letters home since his departure from London. The cadets had endured an all-night journey to Bridlington way up on the east coast of North Yorkshire, then an immediate march in full kit, before being allocated their respective billets. To Joe's surprise, these turned out once again to be rooms in private houses that had been commandeered by the RAF for the duration of the war. As was common with many towns and cities in the UK at the outbreak of the war, thousands of Bridlington's citizens had been asked to vacate their homes and hand over temporary possession to the armed forces, for which they would be financially compensated. In this case, it seemed that quantity had taken precedent over quality in the selection of properties for aircrew occupation. An old-fashioned seaside town on the blustery Yorkshire coast, Bridlington's sea front was dominated by old guest houses. The large numbers of bedrooms they contained presented ideal accommodation for the billeting of the large throughput of young men. Joe found himself assigned to a cold, scruffy attic room with a new roommate.

This was expected to be a six-week placement, where the men would receive intensive training that was designed to ensure their fitness as well as a thorough knowledge of the basics of RAF life. By the end of this period, trainee airmen would be hardened. They would have acquired sound knowledge of weapons and their use, as well as the rudiments of RAF discipline. They would understand how to make a life-saving split second decision by identifying whether an aircraft was friend or foe, and know how to survive if their own aircraft was shot down. A successful pass at the end of this course would ensure entry to the next stage of training for a would-be air gunner such as Joe at the EAGS (Elementary Air Gunner School).

Olive was, for the first time since Joe left home, anxious for his wellbeing. He had described the living conditions as 'filthy'. There was no heating, and since coal was only delivered once a month, if you happened to arrive (as Joe did) when it had all been used up, you were clean out of luck. Their paltry allowance of just four shovels of coal (which was to be shared between no less than seven rooms) seemed, to her, woefully inadequate. It was winter-time and the windy North Sea coast could be a hostile and cold environment. It made Olive shiver just thinking about it, but as she sorted clothes into the washing basket she could not suppress a reluctant half-smile. According to the note accompanying his returned clothes, Joe and his pal had reportedly employed some resourceful tactics in the pursuit of warmth. In the absence of a single piece of coal one evening, they had 'accidentally' displaced a couple of bannisters from the stairs and then discovered that their cupboard drawer was also unfortunately 'broken'. Taking the view that the kindest thing to do would be to sacrifice these few items for the good of the many, they had stacked them in the fire and burned them. The consequence of their actions, however, became clearer the following morning, when they realised that they had rendered the entire staircase into jeopardy. It now required the most careful of negotiation, especially in the sleepy stupor of an early start. They had agreed to stick to coal by lawful acquisition from that point onwards. Daft lads, she concluded.

Her hungry son was clearly having to work hard for his food. Meals were now over a mile away in a local dance hall, where a makeshift cook-house had been set up. Cadets walked from all over the town from their various billets or lectures at mealtimes, but late arrivals would find themselves out of luck. Be there on time or no food. Three meals per day were served at regular time slots, but Joe was missing the additional 'supper' service that they had grown accustomed to at the ACRC. This period of adjustment meant that within the first few days of arrival in Bridlington, the overriding sensation he felt by early evening was hunger.

Bridlington was no longer the smart seaside holiday destination of choice that it had once been. Many of the well-known leisure spots had been given over for RAF training facilities, including the Spa, where many of the lectures took place. The town had suffered from bombing raids and the aftermath of incendiary devices during 1940–41, leaving several hotels and other buildings completely levelled. Others now had taped up windows and the most vulnerable were covered with netting to ensure that any falling debris was confined. Joe was not in love with the place.

The ITW was a six-week basic training course, intended to give prospective air crew a solid grounding in all things RAF. The curriculum included Morse code, law, hygiene, maths, armament, drill, aircraft identification, and much more. While six weeks felt like a reasonably long time, it was a packed and busy programme. Joe's days started at 6 a.m. and ended well after 6 p.m., after which time he was expected to 'swot' for homework. He quickly discovered that lectures were interspersed with swift and formal marches across to the other side of the town for the next session, since all of their classes were opportunistically conducted in appropriated buildings across sporadic locations such as hotels and public halls. These marches began at a brisk rate of 120 paces per minute (ppm), but were very soon accelerated to 140 ppm, metaphorically indicative of the pressure being applied to the recruits both in terms of the depth of their learning expectations as well as the velocity and intensity with which they would be taught.

Olive felt huge empathy when she read Joe's description of the North Yorkshire climate. Fog, rain, high winds, bitter cold, and epic sea spray were obviously both horrifying and fascinating to the boy from the land-locked Midlands who had few seaside trips under his belt. She was surprised to find that he had quickly become mesmerised by the regular comings and goings of the fishing vessels in the bay at Bridlington and she pictured him studying the brave and persistent men in the small boats under the greyness of the sky and the violence of the waves. She imagined that it might be somehow therapeutic to watch the thundering water smashing high over the sea wall, when your roots lay in an industrial city with little fresh air of that sort.

Joe was working hard but the smallness and sameness of the new town, which had now become known as the 'one-eyed dump' and the lack of comfort and warmth was beginning to get him down. To add insult to injury, the dreaded PT sessions were held on the inhospitable territory of the foggy, winter beach, and as a result of the damp and cold, his health was beginning to suffer. A lingering cough had turned into a heavy cold and his voice had all but disappeared. His eyes were also now both plagued with conjunctivitis, and he was struggling to see from beneath the sticky ooze, which was driving him mad. Olive knew from the tone of his letters home that he felt appalling. He had reported 'sick' to the MO on at least one occasion so far, desperate for some kind of remedy, which he gratefully took in the form of some kind of colourful draught and a handful of pills. No escape, however, from the daily grind was forthcoming, so he stoically had to grin and bear it.

The frenetic pace of the proceedings was also taking its toll on Joe. At the ACRC he had grown used to the relatively relaxing weekend schedule, where they had worked only until lunchtime on a Saturday, not having to report for parade again until around 8.30 a.m. on Mondays. There were no such luxuries here. Saturday was as full a day as all the others, and Monday's start was early. Any desire for a lie-in on a Sunday morning would necessitate sacrificing a cooked breakfast. Olive was acutely aware of the kind of Hobson's choice that this would be for Joseph, but that, given his current state of health, the lie-in would probably win.

Knowing that Joe was poorly, Olive immediately set about creating a parcel of aid for her son. A terrible 'barking' cough had been with him since the first week of joining the RAF and the exposure to the elements was clearly not helping its departure, so cough linctus was top of the list. She moved deliberately about the house gathering boot polish, warm pyjamas, a large supply of cotton handkerchiefs, corn plasters, and a selection of sweets, feeling a sense of relief that she was at least able to do something to ease Joe's burden with a few homely comforts.

Olive climbed the narrow stairs and opened the door that led to Joe's too-quiet bedroom. She raised her eyes to the shelf, which housed his collection of aircraft and RAF related books, largely acquired as a result of his early boyhood interest in flying and his subsequent membership of the ATC. Since this new ITW course was now entering the realms of aircraft recognition, Joe had requested that his mother pick out and send some of the collection by post. She fastidiously selected and wrapped the appropriate tomes to add to her care parcel, hoping that they would help Joseph with his studies.

As a trainee air gunner, Joe knew how significant the aircraft recognition course was to his designated trade. It was simply unacceptable for a gunner to fail this subject; mistakes here would mean that the whole course would be over for Joe. Olive reflected on her confidence that her son's long-held interest in this subject would make it one of the easier things for him to master, and her predictions proved correct when his inherent knowledge paved the way for success in his very first progress test, where he scored twenty-five out of twenty-five.

There were plenty of other subject tests too, including the 'menace' of Morse code. Training in this skillset often took place on the beach with large Aldis lamps, in the dark. The recruits were expected to be able to deliver eight words per minute to pass this test. In spite of Joe's reticence and hatred of the constant staring at a green light, he managed an equally impressive 100 per cent success rate in his Morse test.

In spite of his health, it was obvious from her son's enthusiasm that Joe was suited to his new career and that he was relishing the technical aspects of the course. He described with gusto the firearms training, which, in spite of the pace, he clearly loved. She could feel his excitement about shooting clay pigeons in front of a world champion instructor, and imagined the curses of frustration that would be leaking form his mouth each time he missed. His letters had become a babble of foreign facts about instructions for the Browning .303 machine gun, four-hour lectures on the 'Sten' gun, the .303 rifle, the .3 rifle, the .22 rifle, and the .38 revolver. Olive was blinded by his science and was little surprised to hear him say that some of the recruits had already abandoned the course as they were unable to stand the pace.

Olive was enormously proud of Joe's results and his tenacity. Apart from the negative remarks about the RAF's failure to meet his most basic needs such as the accommodation, health, money, and food, his letters home smacked of optimism. They were peppered with hints that he was studying hard for the many examinations that he faced in each of the subject matter required, and illustrated to a beaming Olive that his enthusiasm for learning his new trade was still strong.

Olive was becoming a conduit for communications between Joseph and the folks back home. As one of twelve siblings, Olive felt duty bound to relay his progress to those members of the wider family with whom she kept in regular contact, in particular her sisters Phyllis and Hilda. They were very close and both felt great pride in their nephew's adventure, and were consequently always keen for news. This was not a simple feat, since her relatives were spread far and wide across Birmingham and the Black Country. It was not only the family whom Olive was required to feed with information. With each letter came a new set of conversations with the neighbours and a whole host of excitement for Dennis, Joyce, and Brian, all of whom were eager for news of their brother in blue. In addition to this, there were Joe's friends, unlikely to be the recipients of regular mail due to Joe's ridiculously hectic schedule, but with no less interest in his whereabouts. Elmdale Grove was a small, close community, and Joe had many friends who had also joined the various armed services in recent weeks and months. Their mothers swapped news readily, and the children of the grove fantasised about their menfolk in their war games in the street.

Among Joe's friends was Marie, a local girl who Joe was very fond of, and to whom he was writing as often as time would allow. Olive was unsure of the exact nature of Joe's feelings for Marie, but did not question him about it, preferring to allow nature to take its course. After all, if either of them had romance in mind, Joe was hardly in an ideal position to carry on a successful courtship, miles from home, destined for who-knows-how-long in Bomber Command. Time would tell, but she was relieved that his absence would ensure his focus was on the job he had set out to do, rather than on a girlfriend.

At the end of January, Olive received a letter from her son that threw her into a panic and for the first time presented her with a requirement to censor its contents for the ears of the children. She read the letter several times in order to fully digest the details of an incident that had occurred the previous week during one of Joe's armaments lectures. In an utterly matter-of-fact tone, Joe related that a fellow cadet had been killed on the spot in the lecture room when a live round (which some fool had stolen from the firing range) had been put into a magazine. The firing pin had been innocently released and, as Joe put it, 'the fellow went out'. This was apparently not an isolated incident by any means. As if pre-empting his mother's inevitable reaction, Joe reassured her that he was watching his step and would be as vigilant as possible.

Olive was horrified. She wrote back immediately, expressing her deep concern for Joe's safety and supplementing her usual parcel of washing with the only piece of motherly comfort she could offer from such a distance, a homemade cake. It seemed like a silly and inadequate gesture, but at least she felt as though she was doing something in support. She knew full well that she would receive nothing but reassurances and platitudes about the incident concerned, but maternal instincts forced her to place a virtual protective shroud around her son and, if she could offer nothing else, at least she could provide home baking. She knew that she would have to put faith in her son's common sense and reassured herself that, while ever the letters kept arriving, all must surely be well enough.

Less than a week later, however, she received a pencil-written letter from Joe that made her hands shake so much that she had to reach for the back of an armchair to steady herself. Joe had been on a recent successful, but not uneventful visit to the firing range, during which the cadets had fired ten rounds each with a rifle and a further twenty-four rounds with the .38 revolver. The latter would be the first issued weapon that the men would receive when they reached their units, so the higher volume of shooting practice was intended to give them the opportunity to get to grips with it. Joe had been chuffed with his placement of third in points on the rifle and had then moved on to the revolver work. The recruit adjacent to Joe had handed him a weapon for unloading, claiming an inability to complete the task himself. The safety conscious Joe had tutted but made sure to question whether the chamber of the weapon had been emptied of ammunition. An affirmative response was forthcoming, so Joe had proceeded to 'break' the revolver. At that moment, it became abundantly clear that the chamber of the gun was loaded, and he was immediately incensed by the realisation that a less than careful approach to the task could well have resulted in a disastrous injury, or worse.

Although a little shaken by the incident, Joe was far more preoccupied with his furiousness at what he perceived to be the utter stupidity of the other recruit and some of the other men he was encountering on this journey. Unlike Joe, there were those without an ounce of good judgment, or without enough grey matter to keep up with their studies. Some were falling well behind, and although no intellectual himself, Joe was determined to get through whatever the RAF could throw at him, in spite of his illness, the east coast gales, or even attempted murder.

Olive's yearning to see Joe increased ten-fold with the thought of his endangerment, and the news that he had now also been issued his battle dress made her long to see him. He had reported its relative warmth and comfort, but all she could really think of was how handsome he must look in it and how symbolic it seemed of the combat that lay ahead.

The twice-weekly ritual of letter writing was becoming more and more vital, and she had begun to engage the children in contributing to the news they sent to Bridlington. The children asked for a photograph, and one finally arrived in mid-February. Joseph looked every bit as resplendent in his full battle dress as they had all imagined. It had been a tall order to get a photo in Bridlington, where the only place to get a portrait was a 'posh' photography studio in the centre of town, so Joe managed three tiny prints to be shared or enlarged among the family members who were clamouring for them. Encouraged by Olive, both of the youngest children wrote their own letters to their brother. Joe was significantly impressed by the letters he received from Joyce and especially from little Brian, who at eight years old had penned a delightfully formal note, unassisted, enquiring about Joe's virtually nonexistent social life. Save for a single trip to the cinema (the latest 'picture' being *Five Graves to Cairo*), Joe's ritual was work, sleep, eat, and repeat. Besides, he had told Brian, at a 'bob' a time, he could ill afford it. He was, he had confirmed, missing music terribly, since he had not listened to a radio since the day he had left home.

Olive filled in Joe on the rest of the family's activities. Dennis had just got his first job, and at fourteen years old was less enthusiastic about writing letters. He was far too interested in football and money to set aside his leisure time for what he saw as something close to school work, much to his mother's disappointment. He had begun working as what Olive loosely described as a 'wallpaper basher'—a painter and decorator's apprentice, which suited him well. It was physical and varied, and he seemed to be enjoying it.

All this correspondence simultaneously presented Joe with pleasure and dread. He loved receiving news from home, and devoured the letters that came almost daily from various sources, while at the same time presenting him with endless replies to compose and very little opportunity to write them.

As the weeks went on, the finances became tighter and tighter for Olive. Although she received a voluntary allotment that was deducted from Joe's salary each week, she was struggling to support the family on this and her wage alone. She had applied for a Dependant's Allowance, which, if granted, would provide a small supplementary income for the family, but despite a number of enquiries, she had as yet received no response. This was a great worry to her, and she would, reluctantly, have to ask Joe to intervene if a satisfactory outcome did not happen within the next couple of weeks.

The intensity of the course was crazy now. Joe was constantly surprised by the amount of technical content and detailed information he was expected to learn and retain, and the harshness of the physical fitness and safety exercise that they endured.

On the very occasional evening that the recruits had free time, it was invariably spent getting broke—not in the pub (where they rarely had to buy a drink, thanks to the generosity of the locals), but in a little recently discovered café where they sated their unquenchable appetites with cheap, filling grub. Real fried eggs and chips were well worth the expense as far as a growing eighteen-year-old lad was concerned, and Joe and pals were no different.

Olive was getting to know the gang with whom Joe was now friends—Den Maycock from Reading, 'Smokey' Joe Lee, Joe Lyons (also from Liverpool), Stan Dunne from Walsall, and Ken Dilworth from outside Manchester. She was bemused to hear that the abundance of 'Josephs' at the ACRC continued at Bridlington and that 'Mac' had become a helpful differentiating nickname. She, like him, had no idea why 'Mac' was his chosen label, but he seemed to be accepting it with good grace and so, therefore, would she.

The RAF dentists continued to have a field-day in Mac's mouth. He now had no less than ten teeth earmarked for attention, and the prospect of weekly perdition in the dentist's chair until it was all done. The torture would take the form of ten silvery fillings, each of which would be encased in the special lining material that would enable the teeth to withstand the extreme cold and high-pressure environments that Joe's mouth and the rest of his person would be subjected to.

By the beginning of February, speculation among Joe and his friends had begun on the subject of which station they would be sent to at the end of the ITW in March. Joe was hoping that the destination for his AGS (Air Gunnery School) assignment would be Bridgnorth. This was one of two potential locations, and was the one preferred by Joe because of its proximity to Birmingham, being only approximately 30 miles from home. A week later, to his delight, his hopes were confirmed. Bridgnorth was to become a combined ITW and EAGS location, while Bridlington would be turned into a station specifically for the training of wireless operators from now on.

Olive was naturally delighted with this news, although slightly concerned that Joe had informed her that the change of Bridlington's use was a military secret. Was that a joke, or not? Her son still had the infuriating ability to keep her guessing with his sense of humour, it seemed. Knowing that Joseph would be within 'spitting distance', for some weeks at least, was incredibly comforting. Her increasing concerns about the conditions in which Joe and the other recruits were living in Bridlington would hopefully abate once he had moved on. Things there had got so bad that an entire row of four-storey houses being used as recruit accommodation had been condemned as 'unfit for human habitation' in recent days, she had heard. It was said that, out of a Flight of fifty men who had been lodged in these houses, twenty-five were now in the sick bay with everything from colds to bronchitis. Like Joe, the men scavenged wood and coal from wherever they could, chopping it in their billets. It was not unheard of for the downstairs neighbours to be surprised by a shower of lath and plaster during these chopping incidents, but they were quickly getting used to all that. A move could not come at a better time as far as both mother and son were concerned.

Olive passed on the doubly exciting news to the children that their big brother was now entitled to a full five days leave before moving to his next location, which was met with smiles. They were all really missing Joe's happy-go-lucky nature and, to some extent, even his regular sibling torment, even if it did mean that Joyce could look forward to a spell of being abandoned on the roof of the hen enclosure without her shoes.

The ITW course, however, still had to be completed and it was hotting up. Joe crowed about his test performances, scoring 100 per cent in another aircraft recognition exam. Although weapons were fast becoming his favourite subject, Joe was simultaneously fascinated but confounded by the complexity of the Browning .303 machine gun, which was to be the primary tool of his new trade. With approximately eighty different parts to the gun, there were different shapes and projections on those parts that all had a name and performed a certain task. Joe was expected to learn and retain such names as 'sear spring retainer' and 'keeper frost' as well as a multitude of others. He was finding it the most complex of subject matter.

The greatest of importance was attached to such rituals as 'Dinghy Drill' as well as to other aspects of air-sea rescue, for obvious reasons. Recruits were known to be expected to be able to jump (wearing a freezing cold and soggy 'Mae West' buoyancy aid, which had been rotated through several other trainees who had already been in the water) the 15 feet or so from the end of the stone pier in to the uninviting grey North Sea, thus simulating a potential exit scenario from a ditched aircraft.

Even the most uninitiated of men could hardly fail to notice that the incessant rounds of lectures, daily PT, and practical work were designed to craft the cadets in to the kind of hardened physical and mental condition that would be crucial if they were ever to withstand the kind of strain to which they may be subjected as a shot down bomber crew.

A typical mid-week PT session called for Joe to strip to the waist for a 7-mile run in the pouring rain. The 50-mph gales and terrifying waves that hovered up to 20 feet above the main road on the sea front had finally made conditions so inhospitable that the leading officer had relented and the airmen had been spared the last 2 miles of the ordeal. Thank God that Olive had sent cake. She would bake another this week and hope that it got there in one piece.

News reached the family back home that the station had played host to a visit from General 'Monty' of the 8th Army in February. He had visited some of his men, it was said, mostly from the Tank Divisions, bearing the Africa Star. Joe was clearly struck by the popularity of Monty with his men, who seemed to worship him like a god. Joe had looked on as a crowd gathered behind the Bridlington Town Hall building. The General had stood in his Jeep and ordered the men to gather in a square around him. Such was the exuberance of the soldiers around him that he was forced on to the bonnet of the vehicle to speak. This made a lasting impression upon Joe, who was bemused by the reverence and esteem in which these men held Monty. There was perhaps a great deal about the sense of camaraderie and importance of leadership induced by active operations that the novice airmen had yet to learn, pondered Olive.

By the time Joe faced his final ITW exams, he had little to worry about. His hard work had paid off and he was getting consistently high marks in all subjects, passing with relative ease.

Olive took delivery of her skinny, taller-than-when-he-left son and his very substantial kit allocation on the evening of Friday 25 February 1944 for an unexpected bonus of seven days' leave. He was greeted with enormous affection and a hearty stew, which he demolished in record time, after presenting his mother with a wide grin, a large bag of washing, and news that he had lined up a 'date' for Sunday. It seemed, Olive mused, that little had actually changed after all.

1/

Same Wed:

Dear Mom & Kids,

I must first apologise for not having written to you just lately but we have had one hell of a time for the last four or five day's. I've just been writing letters, five of the B——! I think I told you that I had 2 P.O.'s last week, (one from 4 Pearson St & one from Bent St.), well today I recieved another one from Aunt Em' for 5/- again! I must say it came in very useful as I was almost skint after paying for those photos. They will be ready on the 15th Feb, there's only 3 & they are

2

not very big but if I
need to send many around
it will be cheaper to have
enlargements or copy's made,
than to have a lot of the
origanals. This letter by the
way is answering both
the last Wednesday's letter
and the one in the parcel
I must thank you very
much for that now while I can
the cake, by some miracle,
was hardly touched! The
chocolate was a real surprise
it's just the sort of stuff
to have in one's pocket on
an afternoon as we finish
dinner at 12-30 and don't
get tea till 6 or sometimes
after. The crisp's are worth

3/

about 1/- a bog in this
billet." About that Austin 18f,
you had better keep it and
when I send you the photo
you can use it to get
some copy's with. I have
tryed to get an interview
with the C.O. but am told
that he has left for
Bridge-north to prepare
the way for our Squadron.
Yes, it's a "cert" that we
are going!!! We will
finish of our course here
and get our leave O.K.
Now to answere the 2nd
letter, first of all many
of the very best on your
anniversary I'm afraid thats
the first time I've wished

4/

it to you, but you know
just how self-centred I am.
"Please give Den a "kith"
for me and tell him to
use "Amami"! How strange
that a "Perry party
should go off well!? I'm
afraid I must make a couple
of requests while I think
about 'em, can I have some
razor blades and also that
black pen of mine the one
with the nib like a hook.
Lord know's where it is
but Den or one of the other
may have spotted it. We
are in a bit of a mess this
week of over our dirty
laundry as the sergeant
said, "We've 'ad it!" If I don't

5/

get mine done I may send
it home if it's OK. with
you. Anyway lets leave it
at that for a while as
there are about 46 of
our flight who have not
had theres taken either
so they may do summat
about it. I must write
something about our course
now in case you are
interested, the Morse is getting
to be a terror with
some blokes here and I
find it a bit of a bind
as well. The constant staring
a that bright green or red
lamp gets on ones nerves and
after a while ones eyes
go a bit wonky. The next

is the Browning ·303 m.g.
which I find interesting but
darned hard just the
same! There are # about 80
different parts to the gun
and the different shapes
and projections on those
parts all have a name
and do a certain job! the
mechanism is easy enough
on its own but when
we have to remember
such names as, "sear spring
retainer" keeper post," we
find that a bit of a bind
also! Anyway I'm enjoying
the course!! By the way
we get issued with another
kit bag here for flying
equipment, boots, helmet +

7

and goggles etc! We've
seen some of the blokes
from the old "Intakes" with
this second **Kit-bag** on
their way home for leave
and what with full pack
respirator at the alert,
gas cape rolled at the neck
and 2 Kit-bags they
sure looked heavy!! I
think you'd better send our
kid to help me! Oh! I
knew there was summat,
on Tuesday I saw General
"Monty" of the 8th army,
he was here to see some
of his men, a large number
of which are "Tank" men all
of them having the
Africa Star and sometimes

8/

others aswell! He is
a very popular chap with
his blokes, they seem to
worship him like a God!
He stood in his "jeep"
and told them to get in
a square around him
whilst he spoke. They
almost mobbed him, so
he stood on the bonnet
to speak! By the way if
you are wondering why
we are going to Bridge
north it's because they
are going to train all
the Wireless operators here
and make B—nth an I.T.W.
and Elementary Air Gunners
School combined. That
is a military secret so

9/

please don't let it go far. I'm afraid that's all for now ~~~~~ so I'll sign off before this nib gets _to hot!_ God bless,

P.S. Only _16_ more days to go!

Cheerio and love to all

Vern

P.P.S.

This is darned good cake!

Peeling Potatoes

Mac
No. 1 EAGS, Bridgnorth, 'A' Squadron
5 Flight, 44 Course
4 March 1944–8 April 1944

Mac arrived at Bridgnorth the following Friday evening where, following a relaxing week in front of Olive's warm hearth peppered with 'dates' with Marie and a good deal of catching up with friends and neighbours, Joe felt refreshed and ready to get back to it.

He reported for duty at the little town in Shropshire on 4 March at 3.10 p.m. An unpleasant 2½-mile march in full kit and kit bag was their first order, but Mac was relieved to find his bed comfortable, and a vast improvement on the previous offerings of Bridlington. It was also a metaphorical million miles away from the east coast gales, for which Mac was eternally grateful.

Accommodation was in huts here, and there were fires inside for warmth. The camp was surrounded by 5 miles of barbed wire, indicating its substantial size and spread. Initial impressions of the all-important food, however, were not good, and the discipline appeared to be excessively strict. Mac braced himself mentally to tolerate a full six weeks of this new regime, with the prospect of a week's home leave dangling like a carrot at the end of the course.

This was a school for Air Gunners, but there would be no sign of aeroplanes for Mac. Bridgnorth's main attraction as a town appeared to be the fifty-seven pubs which it had to offer its inhabitants and visitors. The camp's saving grace for the newcomers was that it had its own cinema and a small dance hall. At least that was something to look forward to, and for the boys arriving at this new posting, a social outlet seemed vital.

The recruits were put into Flights and Squadrons right away. For Mac, 'A' Squadron, 5 Flight, was his destiny. The Flight Officer under whose command Mac was to find himself had an impressive pedigree and the stories about him which were doing the rounds were fascinating. Norman 'Digger' Williams had been decorated with the Conspicuous Gallantry Medal and no less than two Distinguished Flying Medals. His air gunner credentials and Australian background made him an idyllic officer, and Mac felt good about being in his capable charge. Williams had been part of the famous Pathfinder Squadron, and had already completed sixty operational sorties over Germany before he was forced into a grounding due to injury. Already credited with the downing of twelve aircraft and a further ten 'probables', he had eventually found himself in a dire situation on his last outing. Taking heavy enemy fire, Williams lost half of his turret and had taken a total of seven bullets to his left leg, yet still managed to shoot down two enemy aircraft before the crew limped back to base. This incident had been the one which had earned him the Conspicuous Gallantry Medal. While he had been in hospital recovering from his wounds, the rest of his crew had been shot down over Germany and captured. Williams had found himself at Bridgnorth as part of a compulsory six-month stand-down, and he was cheesed off. Adjusting to life on the ground was difficult, and he wanted desperately to be back in active service again.

Mac was spellbound by these stories and the inspiration did not stop there. The majority of the instructors at the station had completed at least one tour of duty and were decorated in some way. Mac's sergeant instructor, who went by the name of Frost, was also making a big impression upon him. Some stealthy snooping had turned up a rumour that Frost had also been shot down in enemy territory, but managed to find his way back to England without being captured. It was said that he was the only member of the crew not to have received the DFM for the incident, the apparent unfairness of which irritated Mac immensely. Desperate to know more about Frost's story, the recruits had quizzed him, only to be told that he was sworn to secrecy about how he evaded capture until after the war. This intrigue only fuelled Mac's appetite for learning more about the veteran heroes under whose tutelage he now found himself.

The exceptional discipline in camp was tedious. Men were being put on charges for the most minor of infringements. Surprisingly, however, the highly decorated Flight Officer 'Digger' Williams took a more relaxed tone with the men, pooh-poohing their salutes and telling them not to 'act the goat'. He was happy in his declaration that he did not care a damn for formalities, but wanted only to improve the conditions and food at the station for the benefit of the men working there.

Joe was doing his absolute best to keep up with his letter writing. A flurry of correspondence arrived for him in quick succession, mostly sent on from Bridlington, and mostly from young ladies with whom Mac had made acquaintance during the few short weeks he had been there. Joe was a handsome boy, and it was not difficult to see how the combination of his uniform, thick wavy black hair, and wide smile could make a swift impression on the fairer sex. There were signs that this may not all be quite as fun as it seemed, however. Keeping up with the correspondence was difficult enough, but making sure he got his stories straight was quite another. Referring to it as his 'fan mail', Mac noticed that he had not heard from either of two of his more regular admirers, Marie or Alma, for quite a few days.

Perhaps, he quipped, he had put their letters in the wrong envelopes! No doubt he would soon find out. Joe barely had enough fingers to count all the names of his 'pen pals'. In addition to Alma and Marie, he could now count Pat, Yvonne, Mary, and Jean among the various female attractions that seemed to come with a life in a blue uniform. His wavering attention had not gone unnoticed by Marie, and Mac was wary of her replies, since he knew he had been blowing hot and cold of late.

'That' letter from Marie arrived a week in to his stay at Bridgnorth. He felt a small surge of unwanted adrenaline as he opened the delicate envelope, wondering whether this would be the last correspondence with her, but in spite of his misgivings, the letter was entirely amicable. More than amicable in fact. Her neat handwriting was full of cheer and more than a little affection. Quite what he had done to deserve it he could not say, but he certainly felt satisfied with himself.

Bemused by the kit reissue that took place within the first week of arriving here, he listed what he was now required to carry, as if to justify to himself the growing weight of his kit bag:

1 electronically heated outer flying suit
1 inner, quilted, silk-covered suit
4 pairs of gloves—chamois, wool, silk, and leather gauntlets
1 leather helmet
1 pair of suede, fleece-lined flying boots
1 pair of goggles with tropical lenses as well
1 oxygen mask
2 pairs of socks to put in flying boots
2 pairs of woollen long socks.

The recruits received instruction in how to wear all this equipment to best advantage, but the thought of climbing in to the tiny turret space with it all on or about his person seemed almost ridiculous. He had been informed that there would be a whole lot more to follow at his next camp.

By now, Mac had established a firm friendship with his Liverpudlian pal, Smokey Joe. A stereotypically cheeky Scouser, he was always pushing the boundaries of what was acceptable and appropriate in the eyes of RAF 'law'. A bit of a loveable rogue, where he led, Mac followed. If you were still hungry after eating your meal, you simply followed the confident Smokey Joe (assuming the orderly sergeant's gaze was averted) to the back of the queue and went in for seconds, and even thirds; if your hut was short on coal, you simply grabbed a bucket and followed the nonchalant Smokey Joe on a coke/coal thieving outing. They were not the only ones, of course. It was not unusual to get back to your hut with a haul of 'pinched' coal, only to find that, while you had been out thieving, your own supply had been stolen. A borrowed chair from a neighbouring hut was rarely sat upon before someone found a better use for it as kindling—and so it went on.

Fatigues were assigned regularly and generously, and unsurprisingly, the Cook House fatigues were most popular. It was common practice to use this opportunity to 'collect' excess items of food for onward sale within the hut. Sausages, margarine, tea, cheese, evaporated milk, loaves—often the best meals at camp came from the pilfered remains from cookhouse fatigues.

Joe's first cookhouse duty did not go entirely according to plan, however. He was put in charge of the potato peeling machine alongside another of the 'ACRC 6', Joe Lyons. Since they did not fully understand how it worked, Mac and his buddy could only improvise in its use. Their first experiment involved throwing, batch by batch, a massive 10-hundredweight (500-kg) volume of spuds into the revolving drum and waiting for ten minutes to see what happened. Success! The finished vegetables shot out of the end of the drum like machine gun bullets, peeled and shiny white. For some reason, however, which the distracted Joes were unable to adequately explain, the next batch was left in for a full twenty minutes. Upon inspection at the end of this time, Mac was disturbed but highly amused to find a trickle of tiny pea-sized white potatoes spilling pathetically from the end of the machine into the pot. The corporal was less amused, but they somehow managed to escape without punishment, in spite of the wastage.

The long days were turning now into weeks, of which Mac had originally understood he could expect to spend at least six in Bridgnorth, probably without leave. News was now reaching them that the course may be reduced to as little as four weeks. Mac really cared only about leave. The RAF were keen to move the young men on to their operational squadrons as quickly as possible now, so he hoped that leave would come sooner. The programme of training was being condensed into just four weeks, accelerating the tuition and examinations accordingly.

The course continued apace. Mac was excited about the prospect of time on the Range with the Browning machine gun, since this was what he would need to master in the air at the next training station and on active operations. He was thrilled by the noise and the speed of the Browning's fire. Twenty bullets per second rendered the machine gun red hot after a few bursts, and the cacophony of noise that pierced his ears when three or four guns were firing simultaneously still rang in his head a day later.

The highlight, however, was his first outing in a gun turret. At Bridgnorth, Mac took his first step inside the tiny Perspex booth that was to become his home from home for the foreseeable future. They were trained in grounded turrets, which were safely affixed to *terra firma*, but were nonetheless exact replicas of those that a gunner would find in his aircraft. To Mac, all of this was a marvel and reignited his enthusiasm for his work.

A new subject was also added to the curriculum at Bridgnorth. 'Pyrotechnics' would deal with the range of signals and coloured beacons that a crew would be likely to encounter during night flights. Although Mac was looking forward to the new subjects, he knew his weaknesses. Morse code was among them, and the prospect of being tested conveying six words per minute by Morse was not something he relished. Lord knows, he could barely speak at that speed, let alone tip-tap.

At the end of March, Mac received a letter from Olive, which brought him down to earth with an almighty bump. It contained the tragic news that Sidney, the brother of Mac's best friend and neighbour, Stan Clarke, had been killed in action. Sid left behind a wife and a baby daughter, a bereft mother, and brother, Stan. Mac was deeply affected by this news. Death from war was now uncomfortably close to home. He both knew and respected this man, and he felt sick with the knowledge that he was gone. The two brothers had always plotted and planned about their future ideal of a life in Canada once the war was over—a dream which would now be confined to the past for Stan. Mac reeled at the thought that Sidney had gone. It felt as though he had only seen him yesterday. He wrote Olive, asking her to mail photos of both brothers from home, and he penned a letter of condolence to their mother, Mrs Clarke.

Olive had invited Joe Lee, whom she felt she already knew, to visit on their next leave, and Joe Lee had also set sights on whisking Mac up to Liverpool for a few days, but Mac was torn. He did not want to disappoint Joe or his mum, but there was unlikely to be a generous enough period of leave to accommodate both. His desire to see Stan and to pay his respects for his loss, however, was ultimately overwhelming, although at the same time he was truly lost for what he would say. Mac could only ever remember feeling this way once before, and his thoughts moved to the upcoming April date that would mark the third anniversary of his father's death. He would go home, should the opportunity arise.

Mac learned that there were a possible four locations for the next flying stage of his air gunner training. His next posting would certainly not be in England. The four AGS stations were based in Scotland, Wales, Northern Ireland, and the Isle of Man respectively, and since Joe Lee had a very hospitable cousin in the latter location, the Isle of Man quickly became their preferred destination. One thing was looking certain, it would not be close to home.

The downside of an abbreviated course was the lack of revision time. With exams looming after just four weeks, Mac and the other men had to cram in their swotting when and where they could. The content of the course rarely allowed them spare time, and the usual week of revision time went by the wayside as they found themselves learning new subject material right up until the eve of their exams in the first week of April.

In Mac's case, his customary hard work was to pay off. By the first week in April, the exams were all over and a relieved Joe received the news that he had passed.

A celebration party was held without delay in a private room at the back of The Squirrel pub, one of Bridgnorth's fifty-seven fine establishments. There was, for once, no shortage of food, and Joe allowed himself three well-earned pints of beer and cider, washed down with the same volume in fizzy pop. Never shy of the limelight,

Smokey Joe took to the floor to deliver a witty speech, and the proceedings heated up with a number of drinking games and impromptu 'cabaret' performances from an excitable 'Digger' Williams and Sgt 'Frosty' Frost who had both been invited by the recruits. The latter was exceedingly well regarded by the men who were quick to acknowledge the depth of the learning they had received while in his hands.

This extravagance was thanks in part to the 10 shillings his mother had sent him, as well as the regular pocket money received from his aunts in the form of postal orders. Despite his protestations, the money had kept coming. He was keenly aware that it was a devil for his mum to make ends meet at home, so he was planning a visit to the Accounts Office to see what financial support might be available for Olive by way of a war grant or similar.

The high spirits were ended swiftly when Mac learned that he would not be getting any of the longed-for leave before moving off to Flying School, which was a further six-week course, commencing immediately. A friendly WAAF in Wing HQ had whispered that their next destination was to be Castle Kennedy, near Stranraer on the west coast of Scotland.

She happened to be accurate, and Mac was packed and on his way by Friday 8 April 1944.

Somewhere-or-othe
near Bridge-north
Wednesday

Dear Mom & Kids,
I couldn't mak
it after all as you found
out! They decided to give
us our exams on Monday instea
of Wednesday as arranged. Of
course they waited till the
last minute to tell us! The
exams finished today and I
have passed! Whoopee!!
I will not get any leave
before I go to the Flying
School. We've been told to
be prepared for leaving
on Friday or Saturday. I am
well in with a W.A.A.F &
in the Wing H.Q. & she say
we're off to "Castle Kennedy"
on the West coast of Scotlan

which happens to be a
seaplane base of a sort. The
wonderfull thing is, that
there's an "Ice Rink" at Stran-
-raer about 3 miles from the
'drome !!!!! Just as soon as I get
my new address I want you
to send me my skates + stone
by registered post please, as if
I know of a "Rink" + I can't go
there may be a "looney" roamin'
o'er the glenn's! Blimey I'm goin'
Scotch already!! If I toddle
home in "Thompson Tartan" don't
be surprised! As I told you
we had arranged a bit of a "do"
for Tuesday after the exam's. Well
we had it and I had the
time of my life!! No kiddin, our
flight officer "Digger" Williams +
our Instructor ("bless his cotton
socks") Sgt Frost made the party

3/

go with a real swing. We
had a darned good meal-
Soup, Brawn + pickles, "hot dogs"
fish cakes + chips, with cak
+ buns galore! There was beer
cider + pop, + we could have
whichever we wanted I had
about 1½ pints of beer + the
same in cider then the sam
in pop. After the eats we
had the "wits" of the clas
out to give us a couple
of phoney "speeches", the
one being Joe Lee of cause,
the chump! Digger after
much ragging put 3 ½'s
of beer in line at one en
of the room + 3 marbles at
the other. He the got 3
boobs to role the marble
with their noses down to
the beer as a race! Oh bo

4/

what a mess! Later we had "Frosty" singing us some air-crew ditty's in the real technical way and what a row! "Digger" did a dance of a sort, he called it "Chili-Chili"! We invited a bloke who we all used to know at Brid', to play the piano' and we had a good sing-song and a lark to fill in the time. All those celebrations we had in a big private room at the back of the "Squirrel". No one got sozzled. I wrote to Mrs Clarke (or did I tell you) but I'ue had no answere as yet. If you can find those two photos of (Stan) & (Stan & Sidny) let me have 'em at my new address. Tell Joyce to write to me about her holiday. Hope she's havin' a

good time. No, I haven't written
8, Charles Rd and dont want to
either! Hope you, Aunts Eri' and
Jill have some fun at Easter,
wish I could be there too!
These envelopes have come in
Just right as I've got to write
to Alma, Marie, Pat, Yvonne
Mary and Jean besides that
"Bridge Inn" as they've Just
sent me 5/- from the funds! I
am enclosing that P.O. for
you to send my skates & stone
as I know you cannot manage
it out of your money these days
By the way I have seen the
Accounts bloke but I haven't
had anything in the way
of a real facts off him, but I'm
trying again! I also miss
your faces at home too but I'll
be home in about 6 weeks

PTO

with a "Scotch mist" on each arm! I hope !!! Thats all for now, will try to phone before I leave for Scotland. Now for that fan-mail! So-long

Love to you al

P.S. Excuse the Chinese!

Joe/
x xx x

5

Airborne

Mac
3 AGS, Castle Kennedy, Stranraer, Scotland
39 Course, Hut 13, 1 Site
8 April 1944–26 May 1944

April arrived. Another month and another RAF Station. This one was at the end of an eighteen-hour journey that had commenced at 6 a.m. The 300 miles from Bridgnorth was a tortuous and dreary, epic event under 1944 military conditions.

Mac's stomach was, as ever, the first gauge of whether Castle Kennedy would cut the mustard. Thankfully, the first impressions on that front were excellent. The men were for once greeted not with a long line, but with a super meal, and better still, Mac awoke the first morning to the most delicious bowl of porridge he had ever eaten. While porridge in itself was no stranger to Mac, the welcome addition of both real milk and sugar put a smile on his face. The subsequent fried breakfast of eggs, white bread, and butter with sugary tea sealed the deal. It looked as though the following seven weeks here might be made more bearable by full stomachs.

The course, however, would not commence for everyone who had arrived with Mac. Before any of the recruits could begin, there were venereal infection, FFI, and dental inspections to be endured. Once that humiliation was over, there was an examination of a more tricky kind to pass. Without demonstrating an adequate understanding of the Frazer-Nash turret's hydraulic systems, and his knowledge of the potential stoppages and remedies in the Browning machine gun, Mac would not be proceeding directly to the training programme. A typical rear gun turret was generally equipped with four Browning machine guns and weighed 1,350 lb (612 kg) fully loaded, almost half of which was taken up by the 10,000 rounds of ammunition and its accompanying paraphernalia. Spare ammo was stored in four boxes, which were positioned in the fuselage. These were connected to the turret by a series of tracks, each carrying 600 rounds. The feed to the guns was hydraulic and spent cartridge cases were jettisoned to the rear by a pair of chutes, one beneath each pair of machine guns.

The mid-upper (dorsal) turret that Mac would eventually come to occupy was designed to protect the aircraft from attacks from above and to the sides. It was small, only around 30 inches in diameter, and it moved both horizontally (180 degrees in each direction) and vertically (-45 degrees to +60 degrees). Mac and his fellow gunners controlled the guns using a two-handed control column, but there was no room for parachutes, which had to be left outside the turret before entering. Mac would eventually come to know this turret inside-out and would learn to surrender to the cramped cocoon by allowing his boots to enter first, with feet following close behind. Once inside, there was no leaving until the bomber returned to base.

A 'pool' of men would be accumulated from those airmen who did not pass this initial exam and would require further intervention, they learned. No one wanted to be in the 'pool'. Rumour had it that it carried with it the promise of fatigues all morning and a whole week's further remedial instruction to boot. The announcement of the winners and losers was made symbolically after a comforting three-course dinner. Many a finger was crossed beneath the tables as Smokey Joe and Mac both heard their names called out. Passes for both, and progression immediately to the start of the course proper.

The best news was yet to come. Finally, there were runways, and with runways came aircraft! Flying was to commence the following week, and the Avro Anson was to be their allotted aeroplane. A twin-engined aircraft, the Anson had become the RAF's primary trainer vehicle for all bomber crew. It was equipped with gun turrets and a capability to carry up to 500 lb of bombload, making it a perfect base trainer in which pilots, navigators, engineers, and gunners could hone their new skills.

A gunner needs a target, of course, and for Mac this came in the form of drogues that were pulled by Miles Master II aircraft. Small, two-seater monoplanes, they were aerobatic and were given the task of towing the drogues, which were required for aerial gunnery training. Drogues were banner-like wind socks that were attached to thousands of feet of rope and trailed behind the MMII. Mac was excited by the prospect of the aerial training and the idea of using painted bullets as well as cine film to assess accuracy and success rates after each exercise.

He was once again struck by the expanses of this new camp. Getting from A to B in such a widespread station necessitated a lot of walking, adding only to both his hunger and his lack of time.

Orders were received that men must wear full flying kit on all flying details, instantly sparking speculation that they would be venturing to high altitudes over the Irish Sea. Time would tell. First impressions of the officers was pretty good as far as Mac was concerned, although it was clear that discipline would be equally as fierce as it had been at Bridgnorth.

Further new subject matter also appeared on the agenda. 'Sighting' was anticipated to potentially be a 'sticky' one, as the recruits had not encountered it before this point, but Mac embraced it with his customary enthusiasm for the unknown.

Once again, the 1,600 recruits were housed in huts. Hut 13 was Mac's new home and its location certainly reflected the unluckiness of its number as it was only five paces away from the railway tracks, making sleep a challenge. Several new faces had shown up in the new hut too, including one vaguely familiar one who Mac could not quite place. After a brief introduction to the young man named Ivor who was his new roommate, Mac was astounded to discover that they held contiguous Service Numbers, Mac's 3050664 with his new pal Ivor's being 3050665. A little note-comparing of their respective activity up to this point revealed that they both hailed from Birmingham and that they had joined up at the ACSB on the very same day. Small world.

Castle Kennedy was a muddy place, due in part to the incessant rain, but its ugliness underfoot (compounded by a severe lack of washing facilities) was more than adequately compensated by the views. Beside a pine forest and the beautiful White Loch, whose name escaped Mac for the entire duration of his residency, no airman could fail to be impressed by the lovely surroundings. Situated a few miles east of the town of Stranraer, the RAF base had been in use since 1913 and had provided facilities for postal transportation to Ireland during the First World War, after which it had fallen out of use until the current war had broken out. Scotland, due to its geographical distance from the range of German bombers, had become home to a number of training facilities in recent years, and Castle Kennedy was now dedicated to use as a Gunnery School.

All that was missing for Mac was the opportunity to make the most of the world that lay outside of the station. He had discovered the rumoured existence of an ice-skating rink in nearby Ayr, which made his eyes light up with excitement. No one in the Thompson family had a clue from where this obscure passion of his had emanated, but he was a keen skater and owned his own skates. He had telephoned home and requested their immediate dispatch, along with the accompanying sharpening stone, in order that he may waste no time in investigating the rink once they were allowed out.

Any down-time available was often hijacked at Castle Kennedy by more senior personnel who 'volunteered' unsuspecting cadets into unpleasant tasks. Such was the case when the face of Mac's corporal appeared in the hut one morning, seeking the help of Mac and four or five of his naivest pals for the purpose of hauling some coal. An untimely snort of laughter from Smokey Joe Lee saw him rapidly recruited into the chain gang for his cheek. The colour drained from all of their faces the instant they were told that the awaiting lorry would need to be loaded, delivered, and reloaded a total of eight times before they were free to go. Once this first task was completed, they were to be put on coal bag filling duty. It proved to be one hell of a workout, as well as an amusing anecdote to send home.

News coming in the opposite direction had been woefully slow, however, and when it finally came, it had both delighted and worried Mac in equal measure. Along with a note from Aunt Doris had come a surprise Postal Order for 10 shillings, mysteriously remitted by a pub called The Albion Inn in Brierley Hill, in the Black Country. After further investigation, Mac discovered that the pub was run by one of Olive's lesser-known sisters and her husband. Aunt Em and Uncle Tom had a collection box in the pub into which locals and the pub's clientele contributed their loose change. Mac had now unwittingly become a beneficiary of the loot box and was overwhelmingly delighted to receive the promised regular extra funds. The thoughtfulness of his relatives and the complete strangers who frequented their pub touched Mac deeply.

Along with this good news came concerns for his mother. He had telephoned her once or twice since his arrival in Scotland, but on their last call, the operator had cut them off at the worst possible moment. Olive had sounded appalling. He was unsure whether it had been fatigue, depression, illness, stress, or a combination of all four. Irrespective of the cause, such was his concern that he had immediately penned a letter home to check on his mother's wellbeing, and then spent some hours in a state of anxiety. Being away from home, he was discovering, was all well and good when he was secure in the knowledge that life was good with his family, but being hundreds of miles away when something bad happened was no joke. It exaggerated his concerns that he was not equipped to help either himself or Olive, and triggered a temporary bout of acute homesickness that he had not really experienced before.

Confusion had also arrived in the form of new course instructors. The recruits were finding that some of the information being provided by the new tutors was contradictory to what they had learned up to this point. They were beginning to question themselves and some had headed back to their books for some serious revision, in order to clarify the grey areas. This was exceedingly frustrating, particularly in the knowledge that the course was already tough and time-compressed. It was the kind of pressure they could do without.

Their old friend Dinghy Drill was a regular visitor here at Castle Kennedy, and Mac sometimes felt as though he spent all day getting in and out of aeroplanes, without ever yet leaving the ground. A week into his stay, he found himself on a 40-mile drive to the nearest swimming baths for a new kind of Dinghy practice. Once poolside, the men were ordered in to their flying kits, flying boots, parachutes, and Mae Wests. Provided with a dinghy, they were promptly told to 'jump in'. The entire thing was more fun than intended, due in the main to the presence of the indefatigable Joe Lee, but nonetheless a difficult exercise to master.

The men were getting little or no time off still, but Mac and Smokey Joe did not waste a second of it. Both had secured dates with WAAF girls at a forthcoming Saturday night Station Dance and both had been thrilled to note that the calibre of potential female company at Castle Kennedy far exceeded that on offer during their time at Bridgnorth. Joe Lee, mad as ever, was practicing a tango in Hut 13 as Mac signed off on his latest letter to Brum. God help the ladies of Stranraer.

Mac's first day off actually came a full two weeks in to his stay, but he had not received news from home since the worrying phone call with Olive the previous week. He was anxious about this and now also pretty cheesed off by the disappointing discovery that Stranraer appeared to be a bit of a dump. Making matters infinitely worse, the most torrential of rain had continued to pound them, incessantly drenching the men and their kit, and putting a complete stop to all of the flying that had only just commenced. No flying meant more classroom time, more note taking, and longer days of revision. By the time Mac fell into bed every night, he was exhausted.

When he finally got in to the air again, two days later, he discovered that, after a while, it was actually pretty monotonous. Training was currently aided by cine-camera guns in the air and static turrets at the firing range. The cine-cameras were activated as the gun's trigger was depressed, and films were later played back to the pupil gunners in order to assess their prowess with a moving target. Mac was surprised by his relative efficiency and more than a little proud. His confidence was soon suspended, however, when his guns ran away from him at the range. This episode earned him a newer nickname. 'Massacre Bloke' had managed to make a very sizeable hole in a wall as well as create a perfectly scalloped edge along its top, before he could get things back under control. Perhaps he just needed more practice.

The mid-term test loomed large for the recruits and they were flying quite a lot now. Pilots varied in both nationality and quality and Mac was beginning to learn that his life was in their hands. There were certainly good ones and then there were the others. A Polish pilot had taken Mac and the rest of his training crew up on exercises over the Irish Sea, but when they had reached an altitude of 8,000 feet, he had, for some inexplicable reason, cut the engines. Mac's fear had no time to take hold as the overwhelming and imminent issue had been the fact that his entire body was lurching toward the windscreen. This, however, was nothing compared with the sensation of his lungs trying to exit via his ears as the Polish 'loon' dived to 1,000 feet. Szczelski: a name never to be forgotten, even if Mac could not spell it.

In a separate incident, Joe Lee's crew had encountered a severe storm over the sea and their pilot had facilitated a skilled race back to the aerodrome at 20 feet above the waves. This flying malarkey was not for the fainthearted.

It was not uncommon for incidents such as these (and far worse) to occur during training exercises. On 3 July 1944, just five weeks after Mac would depart Castle Kennedy, an Avro Anson crashed in to the village of Knockneen, north of Stranraer, killing all of the crew on board, reminding all of the pupils just how delicate a process this was.

Time was flying and so was Mac in every conceivable way. Mid-term exams began the first week in May. He passed with decent grades. The final exams were only nine days away, however, and he was optimistic to think that he would soon be fully qualified air crew. A pass at that stage would also earn Mac his sergeant's stripes, so he was keen to do well. With the promotion, however, came the threat of income tax to pay, so he hoped that the pay rise would compensate. Struggling to do much with the available time but swot for exams, he found himself way behind on letter writing. The mail was pouring in from all quarters, but replies were having to wait until finals were done and dusted.

By 23 May, it was all over. Mac was told of his success, 'aceing' the sighting exam (which came as a hell of a surprise) and aircraft recognition. Third placed in aircraft range estimation and holding his own in ballistics and a number of other subjects, he was pleased over all by his performance. Smokey Joe had also made the grade, but the chums now faced the depressing likelihood that they would be sent their separate ways.

On the eve of his last day in Scotland, Joe proudly accepted his stripes and beret, before taking off on two weeks' well-earned leave.

Some Place
Wednesday.

Dear Mom + Kids,
                              I recieved,
(with a sigh of relief),
my skates + stove on
Tuesday! I don't know if
you have written any
other letters besides, if you
have I haven't had 'em
yet! The mail here is very
iregular. As I write this
(in my new pad, thanks!) I am
in the "crew - room" on the
air-drome, waiting for the
officer to tell me and
the rest of my crew to
get into our flying kit etc
We are going out on an
excercise over the Irish Sea

2

in about an hour. We have
got a lot of work to do
this week as we get
some important progress
exams on Monday. It's a mid-
term test. By rights we
should get a day off to-
morrow, I hope!! The other
day we had a Polish
pilot for an exercise, and
he gave us all the
scare of our lives! He "cut"
his engines at about 8,000
ft!! Blimey, I nearly went
through the windscreen
as we lurched forward
and then my lungs tried
to come out of my ears
as he dived to about
1,000 ft!! One of the other

3.

pupils was just
getting out of the turret
as we dived but he got
rammed back in the
hard way, very quickly!
We have been up on
whats called 'cine-camera
gun, exercises and taking
moving pictures of our
target as we pressed
our triggers. We saw our
own films of the target
in mid-air today and
they weren't too bad. By
the way that Polish fellow
is called Szczelksi! Wow!
Joe Lee had a scare two
day's ago, the plane he
was in ran into a bad
storm over the sea and

4

they raced back 'home'
about 20 feet above
the sea if he laughs now!
I forgot to tell you
but I got a letter and
the usual 5/- P.O. from
Aunt Em & Co yesterday
too! It never rains but
what it pours! I shall
try to write her letter
while flying for a bit
of originality (look it up!)
I must close for now as
we have to be briefed in
a short time. Have found
out that we may not be
able to go skating! Ayr is
in a "banned" area! I'm not
sure yet, anyway! So long

P.S. Excuse pencil. Love Jack
xxxx

P.P.S. I was thinking of you and the kids at home on April 22nd. It seems so long ago. Let me have, if possible, a cut-out of that memorium notice sometime please.

6

'Crewing Up'

Olive
16 OTU, RAF Upper Heyford, Oxfordshire
13 June 1944–23 August 1944

Joe was now six months in to his training. A bona fide sergeant, he had bid farewell unhappily to his best pal Joe Lee. Each departed Stranraer having completed their air gunner training, bound for their individual OTU postings. For Smokey Joe this had been RAF Silverstone in Northamptonshire, from where he had corresponded to confirm that he had apparently settled in nicely, noting the abundance of Land Army girls close to his new station. There was, as always, no stopping that boy. In Mac's case, the destination was 16 OTU and a trip south to Oxfordshire. After a short period of leave, he arrived at Upper Heyford RAF station on 13 June 1944.

The OTU was designed to prepare air crews for particular types of aircraft and operations, en route to joining a squadron and commencing active operations. This would be the place where Joe would meet the six men who would keep each other alive over the coming months, and where they would, together, learn to fly as a team, by day and at night.

Oxfordshire greeted him with torrential British summer rain but Joe managed to grab a ride on the local charabanc from the train station, so avoided a soaking. The first thing on his mind was food, as usual, so he was delighted to discover the pots of jam, butter, and marmalade that were waiting for him in the Sergeants' Mess (a destination that he entered for the very first time with a feeling of self-satisfaction).

He had managed to split his time on leave between two destinations. The comfort and safety of home had been his first port of call for a few days' rest and recuperation, where he had been relieved to see Olive in good health and good fettle. She had not been as well as she had led Joe to believe. Daily life was nothing more than a reward-less existence. She missed her husband and now her eldest boy with every fibre of her being, and it was medicine for her soul to have him back, if only for a few days at a time. Her face had been a brave one, and she had spoiled him with attention, hot baths, and food, at last savouring the daily chores that were for the benefit of someone that for once could truly appreciate her efforts.

To her mild disappointment, Joe had apparently accepted an invitation from Joe Lee to explore the sights of Liverpool. While he surely deserved the treat, Olive could not shake the smallest feeling of unwelcome resentment that was nibbling away at her insides. Packing him off with sandwiches, she had wished him a jolly trip and asked him to telephone to confirm his safety.

Mac was gone for only four days, and had returned to his mother's home with a grin as wide as the Mersey itself. In addition to the delights of a few days with Joe and his family, the trip had apparently proven exceptionally fruitful in other ways. The two boys had taken the opportunity to visit a nearby fair on the Saturday after Mac's arrival. According to the Scouse, it was sure to be awash with pretty girls and no one deserved a weekend of fun more than two hard-working sergeants such as them, surely? He had hit the mark on one score, as two delightfully pretty girls had fallen into their laps as soon as they had arrived. Never short of confidence, the boys had struck up conversation and Mac found himself beside a petite brunette who had introduced herself as Jean.

Olive's eyebrows raised as Mac reported with immense pleasure that he had arranged to meet the Liverpudlian girl again and had thereafter spent a carefree and profitable few days dividing the hours between his old friend and his new one (the latter, as he pointed out to Mr Lee, being by far the more bewitching of the two). Jean, Olive heard, really was the most charming girl and Mac was clearly drawn to her. His description of their time together was fluid and detailed, and she had never really heard him talk about a girl with such a thoughtful or sincere tone before. She was, he recounted, petite and dark-haired, with a slender figure and a delicate face. She worked part time as a volunteer in the Lime Street station hall, serving tea to the troops, as well as holding down a paid job in a local chemist. She lived in her parents' home with younger sister, Mary, in the Edge Hill district to the south of the town, not a million miles away from Joe Lee's home. It had therefore been easy for her son to nurture what he clearly hoped might turn into a romance, if he played his cards just right.

The only details that Mac omitted from his report were those relating to the time when he had come to leave Liverpool. He had been caught unaware by his own mood, which had been unusually solemn. Jean had been more than a divine distraction, and he was very hopeful that he would see her again soon. Agreeing to keep in touch and promising to write immediately, they had parted with the most agreeable of kisses. He was not sure why he had not told his mother any of this; perhaps it was the instinctive dread that she might say it was too soon, too young, too wrong a time, but he would have plenty of time for reflection once he was at Heyford.

Once installed at the new station, Mac found himself in the slightly less gratifying company of a great number of Canadians, whose one advantage was that they seemed to share a passion for card games. Not quite the comfort of a girl's embrace, but it would have to do. The men were advised that their flying patterns and classroom schedules would be intense here. They were not misinformed. Flying exercises would be three, four, six, and eight hours in duration, and days would be fully filled with twelve-hour working patterns, pausing only for meals and the occasional sleep. The only attraction would be the food. Mac would discover how to live like a Lord at Heyford, with offerings of roast pork and stuffing and the promise of hot breakfasts as a reward for night flying. Chocolate bars and chewing gum were thrust into their hands before going up, and Mac's belly was at last sated.

This is the place and time during that Joe's crew was formed in the typically random fashion that all crews were thrown together. Given the fatal consequences that may have faced a crew who were ill-matched or could not get along, it was ironic that it was left largely to chance that men of similar interests or tenuous connections might come together in the bowels of a vacuous hangar to form a team with the correct mix of skills and personalities. Joe and his soon-to-be crew were all strangers to each other at this point, and they had no idea of the extent to which the following few weeks would be the architect of enduring and close future friendships.

Joe's first full day at Heyford included another round of inspections, including a trip to the dentist (again). It was hard to believe that Joe had any teeth left to fill, but the dentist (affectionately labelled 'The Butcher' here) seemed to find at least one. The men did not escape the now regular humiliation of the FFI (Free From Infection) inspection either. This was a ritual to which all crew were 'exposed' at regular intervals throughout their service careers, and always after a period of leave. The FFI involved the parade of servicemen in their PT shorts in front of the medical officer who would be seated at a table. Upon presentation to the officer in question, the serviceman would turn side-on and drop his shorts, while the officer visually inspected the young man's private parts for signs of venereal disease. This task would require the aid of the young serviceman, of course, who was expected to move the aforementioned appendage up and down to enable a clear view.

This requirement was all based on the official supposition that, upon release from their RAF confines, young men were prone to rushing out and participating in illicit sexual activity with women of low morals. It is widely agreed that the majority of young RAF volunteers in 1944 did not actually behave in this way, but in spite of the lack of evidence to the contrary, the ritual endured. Films, gruesome and graphic in nature, often accompanied the inspection, as a means to presumably dissuade the young men from sexual activities that may cause them harm and put them out of action.

While Olive understood nothing of the exact nature of this inspection ritual, the open dialogue which she enjoyed with her son ensured that she was fully aware of its existence, and tacitly rather relieved for it. Daily talks with neighbours in the Grove and surrounding streets enabled the matriarchs of the neighbourhood to compare tales about their husbands and sons at war. Mac's friends who had not yet joined the war effort were soon to be signed up. His advice was passed on directly to his mates in correspondence, of course, but Olive was also an important conduit. The real-time advice of an air gunner who had completed the twenty-two-week course that Joe had undertaken was invaluable input for a young man about to make his mark.

The changes to the programme since the war had broken out were significant, having moved to its current, more challenging and intense format. Her closest confidante and support was neighbour, Mrs Terry, whose son Leo was fighting in France. Letters were shared with excitement and trepidation, but if they kept coming, all was well. The occasional Old Time Dancing evening brought the women the release they needed to keep going for another week, and Mrs Terry's wicked sense of humour was a welcome retreat for Olive. She had a warmness of character that Olive felt nurturing, and they both relied upon each other for mutual morale boosts, as well as for practical purposes.

Joe had described to Olive the latest set of new flying clothes with which he had been supplied. It included three sets of woollen long-johns (with which he sounded decidedly underwhelmed), a large polo neck jumper, an oxygen mask, and an intercom. Much to his disdain, he was then required to scribe his service number in white paint on each and every single item of his kit. After a day that had consisted of eight hours of gunnery lectures and ended at 10.30 p.m., this was a task of unspeakable unpopularity.

Olive had said goodbye for what felt like the hundredth time to Mac at the end of his leave, glad that he was a distance from the feminine distractions of Liverpool or elsewhere, but sobered by the prospect of waking the following day and all the days thereafter without a man in the house again.

As far as the fairer sex was concerned, she was fully aware that her almost nineteen-year-old red-blooded boy was attracted to and by members of the opposite sex, but she did not know whether or not to approve of the constant stream of female names that seemed to pepper his correspondence. She had taken it all with the requisite pinch of salt up to this point, tutting resignedly at the two Joes' ongoing antics with serial date-making and 'pen-pal'ing. She had, however, thought that the pretty Marie looked favourite to win Joe's affections until he had written from Stranraer of his attempted matchmaking activities to pair her with Smokey Joe. She had been horrified that her son was behaving inappropriately. Becoming bored of a girl was one thing, but she felt serious consternation about what appeared to be his attempts to now 'palm off' Marie onto the hapless Joe. It seemed ungentlemanly and unnecessary and she told him so, much to his amusement. He had immediately set her straight on the matter, advising Olive in no uncertain terms that she was barking up the wrong tree. Her concerns, it seemed, had been misplaced regarding just who was matchmaking with whom. Marie apparently had a string of friends, all eligible and eager to meet a RAF boy, but all concerned about the specific appearance, height, and statistics of the Liverpudlian man they were being lined up to meet. Marie had been merely the scheming go-between and not the intended date, penning a string of questions to Mac for Joe Lee's nervous response.

That said, Olive was aware that Joe had received a letter from Marie, which he had himself labelled an 'appeal'. The girl clearly had deeper feelings for Joe than he felt in return, and his inexperience left him feeling unsure how to deal with the situation. He was, she was somewhat relieved to note, intending to behave in a gentlemanly manner and had no desire to hurt Marie's feelings, but things were getting a little beyond his level of comfort, and he needed his mother's advice on how to put an end to it, without upset.

Olive was relieved, but more than a little confused. What of Jean, and Alma, and the other young women her son was entertaining by mail and in person? She advised on a swift course of action for Marie. Time to move on there before things got too serious. His newest pen pal, Jean, was now drawing her deeper attention. She had kept her promise, and Joe had begun to receive letters from Jean on a daily basis, many of which included photos for him to keep. He was now prioritising his minimal time in order to respond to Jean's letters ahead of any others. Olive could read between the lines. She could tell that he looked forward immensely to her correspondence, and it was clear from his notes home that she was beginning to emerge as the first and potentially last among Joe's writing companions.

Olive, without any particularly strong reason to be wary, was more cautious about the seventeen-year-old Jean's sincerity towards her son. What if she had a string of other correspondents? Perhaps she just saw her son as a pleasant source of amusement, or enjoyed the kudos of being on the arm of a RAF Airman. She wrote and told him to be careful, immediately regretting her words. Olive was concerned that Joseph was displaying such deep feelings for this young girl so quickly, but if she were honest with herself, it was hard to rationalise whether the forthright opinions she had shared were coming from an instinctive urge to protect her boy from getting involved too young or whether she was actually trying to keep him to herself.

Joe, taken aback by her harsh advice, nevertheless penned a nonplussed response. He had no doubts at all that Jean was the genuine article. He told his mother that she was a 'sweet kid' and that he liked her a lot. He was, he declared, unafraid of the prospect of being one of a number to her. He had most certainly been had like that before, and Jean was not the kind. Time, they both agreed, would tell.

It was a very hot June. The weather was sweltering and Mac was developing a lovely tan out on the firing ranges. While he considered the long sessions in the sun to be the best kind of lazy playtime, the weather was capable of creating dangerous conditions, as Joe discovered to his cost. Olive chuckled as she read that, during a four-hour training period on 23 June on the 400-yard ranges near to the base, Joe and pals noticed that their tracer fire was repeatedly setting fire to the dry, parched grass. Much to the amusement of the onlookers, the fires suddenly got a little out of hand and Joe found himself in a predicament as the lit brittle grass began to spread like a forest fire. Joe and his colleagues apparently took chase, stamping frantically to put out the flames, but such was the unpredictability of the fire that it turned heel and chased them back, lapping high at Joe's backside and giving his fellow recruits a magnificent view of his new 'hot seat', and plenty to howl at for the next few days. More filthy than injured, a good bath and plenty of carbolic soap saved his clothes, if not his pride.

Altitude training began here at Heyford. There were purpose-built decompression chambers in which air crew could be subjected to simulated flying conditions. Crews would spend approximately three hours at a time isolated in the chamber, which exposed them to pressures similar to those experienced at heights of 25,000–30,000 feet. It was a necessary unpleasantness for the men who would become accustomed to the real stresses of high altitude soon enough. For the first time ever, dinghy drill was popular. It now gave the men a welcome respite from the heat of summer. A jump into the cool public baths, fully clothed or not, was surely a better way to spend an afternoon than burning your bottom.

Olive limped from pay day to pay day and so did Mac. He had received a pay rise on receipt of his promotion and had committed to saving the increase for his mother. Ever conscious of her struggles, he offered her the money regularly, and although Mess bills mounted up and had to be paid, he tried his hardest to leave his savings intact in order to contribute to the heavy burden his mother bore. He visited the Accounts Office in order to sign the required forms to enable an extension to the deductions from his wages, which were diverted to his mother. The agreed amount was 3/-, but Olive knew that the RAF took their own sweet time to put things in to place, so her son's regular offers of interim contributions were always put to good use.

Joe's nineteenth birthday came and went without a fuss at both ends, although Olive of course sent a card and her best effort at a birthday cake. He missed home greatly the day it came, as he opened his birthday cards and read the sweet words within. Jean had not forgotten it, and had promised a gift would follow, but he did not have time to dwell upon it. He spent the day learning how to bale out of a 'Wimpy' (Wellington bomber), to which he and his newly formed crew mates had just been introduced. It was a much larger aircraft than the Anson they had trained in at Castle Kennedy, so a great deal of time was spent familiarising themselves with the internal layout of the aircraft, as well as learning the all-important newer dinghy drill routine.

In addition to learning how the plane worked, the crew had an equally significant challenge in getting to know each other. This was more than just a case of personal interaction and social proximity. Each of the crew had a specific and highly skilled role to play, and they realised that the sum of their parts would be greater than the capacity of the individuals who performed them.

The seven-man crew lined up as follows: Harry Warwick, pilot; Alec Stott, navigator; Joe Naisbitt, wireless operator; Bill Perry, bomb aimer; Ivor Turley, rear gunner; Tom Waring, flight engineer; and Joe 'Mac' Thompson, mid-upper gunner.

On each outing, Joe reported, the seven men were now making and comparing notes, getting to know the 'intestines' of the aircraft thoroughly, talking tactics and ideas for evasive action. Each of them was beginning to realise the importance of the others. A pilot who shared the difficulties faced at the business end of the aircraft could only benefit from the perspective of those sitting at the rear, below or atop, with a different viewpoint and a different role to play in the air and *vice versa*. They quickly learned that they could do more than just help each other out. They were now a team and the better they understood each other's needs, the better their likelihood of survival.

Harry Warwick was Joe's new pilot. Joe's admiration for his new boss was palpable to Olive. Harry, as with all pilots, had learned to fly the Wellington using dual controls. His prowess had been such that he had gone solo after just four hours of training, which impressed his crew. The admiration was not only for Harry's professional skills, which were beyond reproach. His ability to handle the enormously cumbersome weight of the Wellington during manoeuvres thrilled them, but he also had a warm, easy manner with his crew, and the 'relaxed' nature of their flying experiences were becoming a thing of legend. It was not uncommon for Harry to fly their bird in time to a Waltz on the accompanying radio while the crew picnicked on coffee and sandwiches at 16,000 feet. From the ground, this would have been invisible, but Harry took it a step further, executing a lilting wave-shaped flying pattern in time to the music, so that any onlooker might appreciate their enjoyment in equal measure.

Thankfully, this relaxed outer façade did not undermine the excellent work that they were putting in as a crew, and their efforts were beginning to pay off in training. Following an evasive action exercise, Harry had proudly passed on to the boys a message of congratulations from the squadron leader. Pursued on the exercise by a Hurricane pilot whose sole job was to try and get a shot at their bomber, he had apparently been completely bamboozled by his own inability to get a single shot on target, a failure which the squadron leader had been quick to recognise as the exceptional work of a great bomber crew. Olive was thrilled to hear, not only of the exciting times her son was having, but also that he had personally played a big part in this particular team success. She could tell by his tone that Joe was very pleased with himself, explaining to his mother that the role of the gunners was to provide the pilot with suggested aerobatic manoeuvres in order to evade fighter aircraft.

Harry's prowess as a pilot was equalled by his authority as a leader. On 21 July, as the crew prepared for a night flight, Harry was warming up the engines while the rest of the boys settled in to their allotted positions. Before too long there was a noticeable smell of burning inside the aircraft. It was not unusual to get a whiff of exhaust smoke, so the crew carried on with little worry. After a few minutes, however, it became obvious to Harry that it was getting worse rather than better, and he immediately ordered the crew to evacuate the plane without delay. His instincts had been spot-on. An electrical short in the bomb bays might have proved potentially fatal for all seven of the by-now close men, had they taken off. In customary style, this incident was laughed off, joining Mac's burning bottom in the regular ranks of hilarity. Over 8,000 Bomber Command personnel lost their lives in non-operational accidents such as this during the war. The risks were incredibly high, even during training, and it was thanks only to the quick reactions of Harry that this event had not been added to those statistics.

During this period, the crews were moving regularly between Barford and Upper Heyford RAF stations for flying and classroom training, alternately. The logistics and practicalities of RAF life were frustrating Joe. He remarked that they were constantly being 'mucked about' by changes in plans, or disruptions to activities at the last minute, and was finding it increasingly maddening to cope with the vast distances that crew were required to walk from one end of the Barford base to the other. All of his fellow crew members had bicycles except for Joe, and by July, he could stand it no longer. Olive went to enormous lengths, aided by Dennis, to spruce up the beaten old crock of a second-hand bike, which belonged to her son.

She then had to pay for it to be 'mailed' to him by train, no mean feat for a woman without a vehicle in which to transport such an obscure package. The bike finally arrived, complete with puncture that Dennis had failed to mend, and, of course, so late in the day that Joe no longer had need of it.

From the detail in Joe's letters, Olive felt that she was getting to know the rest of Joe's crew well, even from a distance and without meeting them. Outside of the immediate seven, he talked about other men with whom he had become pals at each of his various stations, and she decided to demonstrate her commitment to their collective wellbeing by taking in additional washing from one or two of them. No matter how amusing an image it was to think about these young men darning their own socks and spending their evenings ironing, she felt it her duty to relieve them of some of the tasks that better fitted her own skillset. One of her regular customers was 'Kilty', a young Canadian whom Joe had befriended. His gratitude to Olive, a surrogate mother in a strange land, was overwhelming. He was a long way from home, mused Olive, and she would like to have thought that someone would do the same for Joseph had he been posted abroad.

It was a big relief in the Heyford laundry department. When the parcels of fresh clothing arrived at the station each week, there was usually a scramble for clean socks. Mac had begun to cause one hell of a panic with his feet each time he took off his shoes at night; men rushed in every direction for the nearest window or door, so the arrival of Olive's laundry packages signalled a welcome respite for a few days.

The overwhelming emotion at this stage of the game for all of the men was fatigue. They were night flying, or finishing very late in the evening almost every day. The 8 a.m. starts and long days were followed by hours of flying the same night. It was not unusual for Joe to fall asleep fully clothed, simply too exhausted to care. Calls to early evening PT sessions from 6–7 p.m. were now being ignored with a certain degree of understandable contempt.

It was becoming more and more common for crews to experience incidents and near misses while out on exercises, and one such incident impacted Harry's crew on a Sunday evening towards the end of July. Having set out for what was scheduled as a five-hour flying exercise, they were crossing the skies of Taunton in Somerset, heading down toward Devon, when an engine failed. Too far away to return safely to base, they knew that a landing site had to be located as soon as possible. Limping, they made it as far as Teignmouth before desperately locating an aerodrome and putting safely down. Once down, they were grounded. This was an Ops Station, and the men were completely forbidden to leave, which had been an unexpected surprise. No letters were allowed to be dispatched either, so they remained stranded for a full two days until their plane could be repaired and was airworthy once more.

Life on the ranges also continued to be eventful wherever Joe was present, or so it seemed to Olive. Clay shooting offered him an opportunity to put some shot through a farmer's window, necessitating a hasty retreat once the farmer heard the shatter of glass.

In July, Olive received a letter from him asking whether he might bring the oft-mentioned Jean home on his next leave. The request was tentative, she sensed, and she knew that the reason for her son's wariness had been the opinions she had given on the situation. Olive had assumed that he would become bored with the constant stream of letter writing, but that had failed to happen. In actual fact, the girl from Liverpool was winning his heart, and she was clearly very fond of Joe too. She had expressed a keenness to meet his family and learn more about the boy she was falling for. In Joe's eyes, there was no time like the present, hence the request for a visit. Olive begged to differ. Her reservations about the relationship were non-specific and certainly not personal to Jean, but she felt a general sense of unease about her eldest (but still very young) boy getting emotionally involved with any girl at this point in his life. He was about to be thrust in to the dangerous world of war and she most certainly wanted him to have his wits about him when that happened. On introspection, she wondered whether she was reluctant to let him go because of his age, his situation, or for more personal motives. Did she want to have him to herself for just a little while longer? Did she resent the young Jean, a complete stranger and non-local? None of her hypotheses shone a particularly flattering light on herself, she realised, but she could not help how she felt.

In addition to the questions she had about Joe, she had worries about her younger sister, Hilda, who had been advised she was pregnant. Elated after longwinded attempts at conception, Hilda had visited a nursing home to obtain a space for the prospective birth, only to be advised by the doctor there that she was not pregnant at all. Hilda had, of course, found this series of events greatly upsetting and Olive had determined to keep a watchful eye on her. They had decided that it would be a good idea, and doubly beneficial, to send Joyce to stay with Hilda for the duration of the rest of the school summer holidays. Joyce had passed her Grammar School exams and it would do her good to bask in some rest out of the city, while also helping Hilda around her place. Olive had packed Joyce off with a small, neat suitcase, and asked her to write daily, if possible. With Dennis working, Olive found herself now alone much of the time with her youngest, brightest boy, Brian.

It was in this slightly stressed condition that she had written, perhaps in haste, to express her reservations about the prospect of having Jean to visit. She knew that her words would hurt Joe, but she did not hold back. He read her letter with a sinking heart. Although Mac loved and respected his mother with a depth that could not be replicated, he simply could not fathom her reluctance to accept Jean, and was hurt and a little shocked by her reaction. He was not prepared to allow any rift to come between the two women, however, and decided upon flattery as the best course of action. He needed his mother to know that she was still his priority, and that he valued her wisdom. Bringing Jean home would not interfere with the amount of time he could dedicate to his mother. If nothing else, he told her, her opinion on Jean would be useful to him. He strongly believed she was special, one of a kind, not the usual Saturday dance kind of girl who he would date once and never see again—all curves and no sense. If Olive never met her, how could she possibly see what he did?

It worked. With gritted teeth and slightly concerned that she was in danger of pushing her son away, Olive relented, agreeing to a visit from Jean for a few days. This was now, it seemed, Joe's girlfriend, whether she liked it or not, so she may as well embrace it and move on. She could not risk losing her son over anything. She was due a week's holiday from work on 20 August, and with an open mind, suggested to Joe that a day out in Stratford upon Avon might do them all good, since Jean was unlikely to have been there before. Conciliatory in tone, Olive hoped that he would accept the olive branch.

Joe had to set aside his anxiety about his mother and his girlfriend as he set his energy to the three days of final OTU exams, which were coming up at the beginning of the very hot August. He took eleven 'Boards' in total and passed each with comfort. It turned out that the exams themselves would be a whole lot simpler than the subsequent exercise of gaining 'clearance' by each of his course tutors. The instructors were each required to sign off their individual pupils as having passed (or not) each aspect of their training programme. This task involved a piece of paper listing each of the names of different parts of the Training Wing and aerodrome, against which Mac was obliged to obtain a signature from an officer to prove that he had been cleared on that particular subject matter. This sounded straightforward but actually involved miles and miles of walking, back and forth, trying to catch each of the required signatories. As if this was not tricky enough, the dual airbase approach meant that the exercise had to be repeated both at Heyford station as well as at Barford. Nothing was ever simple in the RAF.

The boring last days were punctuated with the promise of a little fun. Harry announced that he had 'obligations' with a sweet brunette in Oxford, so a couple of nights out on the town were forecast.

By the end of August, Mac was ready to move again, this time with his crew.

Basic training, all eight months of it, was finished. He had perfected the art of the gunnery discipline, earned his sergeant stripes, added an in-depth knowledge of working in the air as part of a crew to his repertoire, and was now preparing to transfer everything he had mastered to the formidable base of the Avro Lancaster. Olive's fingers were firmly crossed for the next phase of her boy's big adventure.

Heyford.

Tuesday night

Hello Mon,

How are you? Hope you
haven't been worried over me for not
not having written before; but so much
has happened to me in the last few
days that I'm not sure now that
I'm back here again. Guess you're wondering
what I'm driving at!! Here goes. On
Sunday night we were flying and
were supposed to be up for 5 hrs, but
an engine "cut" over a place called
Tainton in Devon and as we could
not get back to base we had to
land where we could. We managed
o.k. on one engine as far as Teignmouth
near Torquay but that began to get

too hot to last and we made for
a drome nearby! We got down alright
but as it was an ops station we had
to stay put!! I made an attempt to
write from there but we then got
told "that isn't allowed from here"!
At first I thought the bloke was
nuts! The skipper said so!! But there
was nothing we could do as we
were not allowed out At all!! The
food + billets there were real
super and of course we all made
"hogs" of ourselves! The kite was
repaired this morning and we got
back about dinner. No one made
a fuss, anyway it happens like that
every day. One of our kites was out
over the north sea, got into difficulties
and started to bawl out "S.O.S."!!
Hurray for England!!! They got to land

alright. They all do. I went to the
Mess as soon as I could and oh-boy
had I got some mail! There was your
parcel (thanks Mom) and two letters
I had sent to Joe Lee (a fortnight
and a week ago respectively) which had
been returned to me. The G.P.O. people
put on "opened in error and moved". I am
going to try again tonight and see what
happens, he'll think I've forgotten
him. I see he's written you, how is
he? About my leave, well I think
it will be a fortnight or two weeks
perhaps even 14 days! Here's hoping! If
we finish this course on time we
shall leave on August 22nd but
don't "bank" too much on that for
the time being. Knowing how this "firm"
works, I'm not saying anything too
definate. You say you're not too keen

on having Jean at home. Well I can
understand how you feel, 'cos as you put
it she's as stranger to you and she
isn't a local girl. Blimey, I don't know
how too put it. I would like to
have you meet her if only to form
an off opinion of her, it would only
be for 3 days, 4 at the very outside because
I want to spend as much of my time
with you as possible. From what I
do know of her, she isn't one of the
usual type I glide around with, all
curves and no sense. See what you
think. I do want to bring her home
and she is always saying she whants
to meet you. Besides her folks have
invited me to their place. About
money, well on pay-parade three
weeks ago I signed a form for your
allowance to be made to 3/- a day but

on the following pay-parade I still recieved £3 - 17, so that meant it hadn't been knocked off. However I have got the extra and am enclosing it. Please let me know as soon as poss to say its safe. I have an appointment on Thursday 10.20 a.m. at the accounts office so I can enquire again about that money. Will let you know. By the way how is the weather at home? Out here its great. We all tried to go into Teignmouth yesterday for a swim but ——! I asked the skipper if theres a day off due for us at all and he was all "mysterious" and said maybe so you may see me "cantering" up the Grove one of these days!! Heres hoping anyway! I was very glad of the clean socks by the way. I cause a hell of a panic in the room each time I take my shoes off!! There is generally one mad rush for the nearest window or open door every night!!!! I leave the reason to your imagination!!! Well Mom I must stop now as my pen-nib is almost red-hot with having written such a long sermon!! Hoping you didn't worry too much, Goodnight & God bless,

Your loving
Son.

Joe /
x x x /

P.S. Will post some more washing in the morning and if possible will phone but you will know if I do before this arrives. Cheerio.

7

The 'Nibs'

Brian and Joyce
Home Leave: 23 August 1944–2 September 1944
RAF Stradishall, Suffolk: 2 September 1944–17 September 1944

The summer holidays were coming to an end. Joyce had returned home from her escapades in the Black Country with Aunty Hilda, where she had enjoyed the best of times, being well cared for and well fed. In her absence, Brian had lived mainly outdoors, firing ants and jumping the brook, returning home only to be fed, with dirty hands and an unquenchable thirst. Dennis's summer had been football-shaped, he was playing for the YMCA and used every conceivable moment and surface to kick, bounce, and dive until he was exhausted.

The downside of Brian's swallows and amazons' holidays had come in the form of a poisoned knee, however. He was at a loss to explain whether he had been inflicted by a sting, a cut, or a splinter, but his mom had declared it 'infected' and had kept him busy for several days, nursing it with bread poultices and warm baths. He was quietly tolerant of the pain and fuss and Olive praised his brave attitude.

Joyce herself had returned to the promise of a radical haircut, in readiness for the serious business of starting at the Grammar School. Her greatest fears had been realised when Olive had led her to a pre-booked appointment at the local hairdresser's salon, where she had commissioned the removal of her long, thick plaits. In their place came a shorter, more grown up style, appropriate, according to both mother and hairdresser, for a soon-to-be teenager. Both Joyce and Olive felt the loss of the plaits more deeply than either expected. Although she did not say so to her daughter, Olive was filled with remorse for the hair crime for several days, before the loss made way for satisfaction, as they both became more accustomed to the new face in the mirror. The Thompsons, however, clearly bore a strong curly hair gene, and Joyce's new beast was likely to require some serious taming.

Now in her second year at the local Grammar School in Kings Norton, to which Joyce had proudly earned entry following her success in the 11+ exams, she was growing up quickly and had, necessarily, become an independent girl. She was barely able to recall a time when she had been able to walk around without her little brother in tow, or had the luxury of her mom's presence at home when she returned from school. Those days had disappeared two or three years ago, when her mom had taken up a post as a local ARP warden, in an attempt to keep the family afloat following the loss of their father.

Olive's ARP role, in which she was still active, involved unsociable hours. Either she left the house at the crack of dawn for a 6 a.m.–2 p.m. shift, or worked from 2 p.m. until 10 p.m. at night. Since Joe's departure and Dennis's new job had begun, this had meant that the two kids had often to look after themselves. A post-school hike was often called for, as they headed to one of the ARP stations where they would have tea with their mom. One of the two posts that Olive frequented was situated in the back room of Mr Humpherson's butcher's shop. Tea might consist of a couple of rounds of bread, loosely held together by homemade blackberry jam, and would be dished up in laps while the two kids recounted the ins and outs of their day. More often than not there were stifled giggles, as Brian and Joyce quietly observed the frequent revisits to St John's Ambulance first aid procedures, the 'how to' of the fire-damping process, or some other emergency drill. The ARP, it seemed to Joyce, was mainly made up from middle-aged local residents who were perhaps not enjoying the adventure of it all quite as much as she and Brian did. The second of Olive's warden posts was further afield and required a fairly long walk, often in the dark, to 'The Grange'. Brian had no idea whose house it was or used to be, perhaps some ancient squire of the village, he conjectured, but it was bloody spooky. The large house was situated at the end of a long, winding drive lined with trees, where his imagination frequently went wild as his grip tightened on his sister's hand. Inside were what seemed like miles and miles of wooden-floored corridors and dark passageways, providing the perfect conduit for scary fun. Hide and seek in a labyrinth such as this was too good to miss, and he and Joyce often lost themselves for hours while the old folk went about their dreary business of saving Northfield. These games made it well worth the walk.

Most recently, however, Joyce had decided that walking was for fools. She had saved her pocket money until she had enough to negotiate the purchase of a long sought-after bicycle. Second hand, of course, as only the rich could afford decent bikes. Her acquisition was an ancient wreck for which she had, albeit willingly, parted with the princely sum of £1.50. Her mum had been incandescent with anger, cussing the mother of Joyce's friend for daring to extort such an elaborate fee from her young daughter for what was an obvious 'crock' of a cycle. The outrage did little to dampen Joyce's enthusiasm for her new wheels, however, and before long she and Brian were mobile, two-up.

The remaining few days of the holidays were spent in idyllic play. While the weather was not always good, it felt that way, and little could dissuade the children of the Grove from their games of cricket, sardines, or hopscotch. A favourite common pastime was hunting for shrapnel, and Brian had formed an enviable collection over the past year or two. The long summer provided the local children with perfect freedom and time to go in search of new treasures. Word got out that a stray bomb had landed somewhere in a field down by Merritt's Brook, and a gang was duly formed to investigate the scene. Joyce took Brian along with the intention of viewing the crater and scouting for items to add to their collections of Army cap badges and bits of metallic scrap. Pride of place in Brian's display was currently held by a piece of metal from the fuselage of a German aircraft that had crashed on a nearby golf course early in the war. Or so Brian had been informed by the donor of the splendid piece.

These 'finds' were among the few distinct discernments of war that the children experienced. Life with their dad and life before the war seemed like something that must have happened in a dream. They still had their mum, and their bellies seemed always to be full (invariably thanks to Olive's masterful domestic skills) so everything was okay. They had all grown accustomed to not asking for treats because they knew that there were none to be had. A tiny allowance of sweet rations was supplemented by other, more substantial foodstuffs, and the welcome sound of the daily baker's horse, Bob, was always a comfort. Bob was invariably hotly pursued about the Grove by a mother with a shovel and he rarely disappointed. Thirsts were quenched with the arrival of the 'Loose Milk Lady' who dispensed her product from an open churn to the eager messengers from No. 16 and surrounding neighbours.

Other sources of nourishment came from a handful of home-grown veg and the half dozen or so hens, which had taken up residence in the back garden. Their provisions came in a number of forms. Eggs (fresh), retrieved on a daily basis by the dutiful Joyce; meat (occasionally), provided by Olive who was pushed to the front of the queue when a neck had to be wrung to dispatch a tired old bird for Christmas lunch; and preserved eggs (unpopular with the kids), which sat throughout the winter in a bucket of clear jelly-like liquid which they later discovered was water-glass. This wallpaper-paste-like substance stored the little oval treasures well, but was a source of disgust for Brian, who generally deferred to his sister when it was time to extract and handle the slimy by-products. Ever resourceful, Brian's preferred snack had become a concoction of cocoa powder mixed with powdered milk and a little sugar. Poured into a paper bag, to a licked and dipped finger this cocktail was nothing short of heavenly.

On occasion, the sights and sounds of war had come closer to home, invading the senses of the children in such a way as to ensure that they would be forever embedded in their memories. The cold and wet of the home-constructed Anderson Shelter in the back garden was one such device. It had a pungent stench of damp that invaded the hastily installed bunk beds. After so much time, they now bore an inherently unpleasant odour, despite Olive's attempts to launder it away. Sleeping here had become a last resort, but when the air raids had been heavy and the shelter had been new, Brian and Joyce had relished in the adventure of it. Their hearts would skip a beat at the sound of the sirens going off, and they would grab torches and blankets and hurriedly scuttle along the narrow path to the rear of the back garden where the secret den was housed. Sleep, however, had been almost impossible, thanks in the main to the awful cold that had no problem penetrating the metal walls. The months and years had negated the joy of these episodes and the kids had taken more recently to laying out a mattress in the lobby beneath the stairs, where it was warm and the raids were passed in relative comfort.

School had often been disrupted due to air raids. Half days had become common when heavy attacks were anticipated and the teachers, as frightened as the children, provided little comfort on those occasions when they were forced to evacuate the school buildings. Joyce had returned from school one day, keen to tell her mother and brothers how that day's air raid had resulted in one teacher actually creating more of a panic than preventing one. She had apparently gone loopy, rushing children out of the door, and eventually taken to screaming at the top of her lungs behind the exiting hoards that they must get to the shelter. Joyce had turned to see who was responsible for the screaming, but had been baffled momentarily to find that there was apparently no one there. Closer inspection had revealed that the teacher in question was actually on the floor, hiding under a school bench. Brian and Joyce both found this episode indescribably funny, enjoying the idea of a teacher's authority and dignity being reduced to grovelling under a bench in the most undignified manner.

The air raid shelter at Tinker's Farm primary school, which Brian still attended had on more than one occasion provided a perfect platform from which the children could witness the continued attempted Nazi assaults on the nearby Austin factory in Longbridge. Dogfights in the blue skies of daylight raids were riveting spectacles to Brian's young eyes. He was awestruck by the sounds of the machine guns, albeit distant, and he would squint hard to try to identify, generally unsuccessfully, which aircraft was which.

Yet even these close to home incidents did little to really frighten the children, who revelled in the thrill of it all. Their innocence protected them and, like the movies, no one seemed to actually die, or at least no one they knew well had died yet, and the bombs that dropped did not seem to drop in Northfield. This rendered the entire war a kind of semi-fantasy for the little Thompsons, like something that was largely happening to other people.

The never-ending excitement of receiving Joe's letters several times a week could be surpassed only by one thing—his arrival in person, in uniform. He was their bona fide hero, and for Brian in particular, it was impossible to tire of the news that was held inside the tiny envelopes that held Joe's handwritten adventures. Their big brother was now wearing stripes and flying in aeroplanes, which only added to Brian's internal narrative of his brother's fantastical escapades.

It was during this last period of the summer holidays and Joe's most recent home leave that his new girlfriend arrived to visit. She talked with a strangely musical dialect and was kind and sweet to both Brian and Joyce. Jean, as she had told them she was called, had come bearing gifts. Joyce, with wide eyes, had unwrapped a box of *eau de parfum* by Bourjois, called *Soir de Paris*. Transported immediately to womanhood, she had caressed and gazed at it, but not opened it. The treasured fragrance would remain boxed and intact for several months before she dared to pick at the outer cover and sniff. It was an excellent opener, and Joyce was sold on the girl who worked at the chemist shop immediately.

Jean's quiet and polite demeanour was impossible even for Olive to find fault with, and irrespective of her reservations or ambivalence about the relationship up to this point, Olive had welcomed Jean in to the fold with warmth and generosity. It was a relief to her as much as it was to Joe. It had taken her no time at all to educate Jean as to what may lie ahead if their romance continued, demonstrating the efforts and volume it took to feed not only Joe, but a small army of hungry children. A delightful thank you letter had followed a day or so after Jean's departure, sealing the deal on her approval for Joe to move ahead, all guns blazing.

Joe had returned to his RAF duties as Brian and Joyce had returned to school. Neither of the kids had wanted the summer or Joe's leave to end, but it inevitably had.

Joe's new post was the lousiest yet. RAF Stradishall was in Suffolk, to where he made a ridiculously excessive fourteen-hour journey from Heyford. The miserable nature of the place made the end of his happy leave all the more depressing. Forced now to march everywhere in squads, there was a ban on bicycles until after 6 p.m., and the food was appalling. Finding one's way to the nearest town of Haverhill was a rocky prospect too, unless your idea of a good night out involved taking the last bus home at 9.30 p.m. Grimmer still, any ideas of home leave were futile, since reaching Birmingham would require Herculean efforts and a journey akin to a circumnavigation of the globe. The only saving grace of Stradishall it seemed, was the prospect that they would soon be out of it, expecting a stay of only a fortnight to tolerate.

Within a week of arriving at Stradishall, it had been christened 'Stalag 1¾' by Joe and crew. It did not take long for them to deduce that this was a place where they had clearly been sent merely to mark time while waiting for a space to be vacated on the required 'Conversion' training programme. Stalag 1¾ was an aircrew school and its only offering was to provide hour after hour of unwelcome classroom time where the men restudied the subjects that they had already perfected and qualified in. Joe, frustrated, resigned himself to putting up with it for two weeks, knowing that they would then be just a few short weeks from completing their entire training and joining a squadron. Their next stop would be a month at a heavy conversion unit, making the transition to the large bomber aircraft, before finally reaching a Lancaster 'Finishing School'.

The radio, as ever, talked only of the war. The kids still listened every evening with Olive to the news and it was sounding more and more as though it would be coming to an end soon. Perhaps this meant that Joe would be coming back for good, and that the blackout would be lifted? The neighbours were full of talk and speculation about what might happen and Brian and Joyce picked up on the snippets that were exchanged in the Grove. They had become aware that their mom was now one of only three remaining ARP wardens in the locality and that ARP wardens were only required during wartime. They understood that they relied on her income and that Olive worried about it, but they also knew that there were others in the street with similar and bigger concerns. Freda, a neighbour in the Grove, had had little or no contact with her husband since he had been captured and entered a POW camp in

Germany. A recent chance purchase of the *Evening Despatch* last week, however, had presented Freda with an article about a POW football team. She had cried for fully an hour, the children overheard, when she had read her husband's name as the team captain. Such a thrill had heartened both Freda and the rest of the community along with her, who felt her relief as if it were personal to each of them.

Joe Lee was sending occasional news too, and his correspondence invariably provided the family with entertainment in the form of a good belly laugh. His latest did not disappoint in that department, although it also gave them a shock in the form of the story of a close shave. His crew had lost both engines on a recent flight, causing an emergency scramble to a nearby aerodrome. There they forced a landing that could only be made across the runway, having too little height to make a proper circuit and come in straight. The impromptu landing had been executed through the hedge at the perimeter of the aerodrome, smashing the starboard undercarriage and swinging the plane around on its underbelly. In turn, this then caused the collapse of one of the wheels and completely detached the starboard wing. It sounded a fair old mess, but miraculously no one was hurt, leaving a despondent ambulance driver, who, according to the ever-jocular Joe Lee, sulked for days with disappointment at the lack of charred remains to get his hands on at the scene of such a spectacular crash.

Once school restarted, life resumed its steady pace at Elmdale Grove. Olive lived day to day, waiting to learn when her job would end, and resolved to look for new employment in the meantime. The fulfilment of a plea from Joe, however impractical, for an apple pie by post occupied her hands and spare time as she employed the children in a mixing, rolling, and chopping production line. The arrival of a new, more permanent address at RAF Feltwell signalled that it was safe for the pie to be dispatched with hope of actually reaching its intended recipient.

The war in Europe may well have been coming to an end, but until someone said otherwise, life would go about its mundane business for the two smallest Thompsons, who saw no escape from the return to school on the horizon.

Wed.   16 Elmdale Grove
                                    Northfield
                                    B'ham.

Dear Joseph,

Many thanks for letter & I was glad to
see that your parcel had reached you. Your
washing had arrived when I got home from
work yesterday, so it remains to be seen how
long it will be catching you up now that
you are on the move again; anyhow I won't
risk an apple tart in it, as if it is as long
on the way as the rest of your mail it
would be mouldy. I'll risk it as soon as I get
your new address. You sound as if you had quite
a good day when you went to Cambridge (Join
the R.A.F. & see the world!), I hope you didn't let
your old college down!!

I was interested to hear about Joe Lee's adventure
& glad to know he had pipped the ambulance
men. Joyce went — by appointment — to the
hairdresser & had her hair cut properly & now
I'm getting used to it & rather like it, to say
nothing of being less trouble. Brian has had
a nasty poisoned knee, I don't know whether
it was a thorn or sting, but I have been kept
busy with bathing & bread poultices, till
now it has broken & I think it will go O.K.
He's ban a good little kid though. Ian is in
the midst of footballing — he plays for the
Y.M.C.A — & of course takes every chance to get
in a bit of practice. You didn't say what you
had done about your bike, so I've taken it
for granted that you have it with you.
There is nothing more of interest at the moment

I'm still wondering what job I shall get when this is finished. Buster was over this week-

I didn't see him to speak to, but he is still in R.A.F uniform. Percy Jones went back yesterday + he is expecting to go abroad to finish his training. So I'll finish now so that I can go home + get your ironing done + your parcel ready. Cheerio + God bless

Love from

Mother + "nibs"

x x x x.

8

A Funeral and an Engagement

Mac
1651 Squadron, Heavy Conversion Unit, RAF Wratting Common, Cambridgeshire
RAF Feltwell, Nr Lakenham, Norfolk
RAF Methwold, Nr Thetford, Norfolk
17 September 1944–6 December 1944

Under his own pedal power, Mac relocated for what he hoped would be almost the final time, a short 6-mile bike ride from Stradishall. With no transport offered by the RAF for their bicycles, the men had sent their kit ahead and had followed after on two wheels. They were immediately grateful that they had their own transport as Wratting Common was immense. While they had taken no time at all in discovering that the food was good in the Mess, they had also found that a 2-mile hike in each direction across road and field had to be dealt with before they would be able to eat it.

Initially advised that the HCU was to be a month-long stay, Mac was now unsure whether that was entirely accurate. Five weeks' minimum could now, he understood, be anything up to nine weeks, due to the overcrowding of simultaneous courses all running at maximum capacity.

The metal-constructed Nissen Huts, which had briefly made an appearance at Bridlington, were now back, but this time in warmer weather, which rendered them sauna-like during daylight hours and cold at night.

After a day settling in, the crew were sent on a liaison visit to a medium frequency radio station where they were taught the details of its operation and processes. An overnight stay had been part of the deal and this provided Mac with an unexpected delight. The local villages that they passed through on the journey to the radio station at Pulham had street and house lighting, so it was clear that the Blackout had been lifted in this area. He found himself reflecting on not only how beautiful the villages looked with their lights twinkling, but how little he actually recalled of the times before Blackout. Five years in his only-just-adult life seemed like an eternity and he could barely remember how his home town looked with the lights on.

The days here were now filled with boring, but useful revision. Far better entertainment came in the form of Jean's increasingly love-filled letters, to which Mac responded with full reciprocation. He knew that he was falling for the sweet Liverpudlian teenager more and more as each week passed, and he was now tactically ignoring correspondence from any other girls, in whom all interest had subsided.

A cheeky night out of base on the town in Haverhill by bike had seen Mac put on a charge already. He, Joe, and Bill had headed off to the cinema for a spot of light relief for an evening and on their way back into the station, torch-less, they had been stopped by a service policeman who had promptly taken their details, the results of which had not been revealed until a few days later. A trip before the chief gunnery instructor was required, where three days of 'disciplinary work' in the form of square bashing were dispensed as punishment.

On the same day that this bad news was dished out, Mac sat his final exams. The revision had clearly paid off—Mac was placed second overall, with only his rear gunner crew-mate, Ivor, pipping him to first position. He was exceedingly pleased with himself.

A new crew member had now joined the ranks of their small brigade. His name was Tom Waring and he was from Sheffield, joining them as flight engineer. Harry had spent a fair amount of time with him already, since pilots and engineers mostly took their lectures together. With Harry's seal of approval, the acceptance of the other crew members followed automatically. As one new crew member arrived, another was temporarily lost. Bill Perry, the crew's bomb aimer, had been taken quite ill. He was currently resting at home, where he expected to remain for up to a month. By now excellent friends, Bill was missed by all his fellow crew-mates both for his company and also for his most excellent skills as a bomb aimer. His temporary replacement went by the name of Boot, and Mac and his pals braced themselves for a period of readjustment.

With constant talk of demobilisation in the newspapers and speculation about the end of the war advancing, Mac was torn between his own personal scepticism and the never-ending propaganda. In his heart, he found it hard to believe that he would not see at least eighteen months of active service operations. The Japanese had yet to be silenced and it seemed unlikely that the services of his crew and the rest of the RAF would not be required for some time to come.

Personnel changes or not, any thoughts of team-building were called to an abrupt halt in the first week of October when all but one of the entire crew of a Stirling Bomber were killed as their plane crashed after take-off from the base. Harry, Mac, Ivor, and Tom were immediately selected to represent 1651 Squadron at the various funerals of the lost men at locations around the UK. Although Mac's destination had entirely coincidentally been determined as Liverpool, he was now heading there under circumstances that were far more sombre than his usual trips, and of a nature that would profoundly affect Mac emotionally for a while to come.

Harry was to be sent to Swansea to attend the funeral of the crew's navigator, Ivor to Cardiff to pay respects to the mid-upper gunner, Tom was on a train to North Yorkshire and Mac was heading to the home of the crew's rear gunner. He was carrying a letter that had been handed to him by the CO at Wratting, intended for the father of the deceased gunner. He had taken it with reluctance. He was less than enthusiastic about the task with which he had been assigned, but orders were orders. The idea of witnessing the intense grief of a family for a man he had never met filled him with dread, but the CO's adjutant had stared the four men in the eyes and made it quite clear that, depressing or not, someone had to do it.

It was 4 a.m. on Thursday morning by the time Mac's overnight train arrived at Liverpool. His fatigue did not improve his mood. The funeral turned out to be even more hellish an experience than he had anticipated, with his role as squadron representative being tested to the limit. Things had begun badly when the coffin failed to arrive on time, necessitating that Mac run around like a madman trying to find a telephone so that he could contact the railway services and try to express the urgency of the situation. The waiting around had been painful for the family, and Mac had felt incredibly sorry for them.

The deceased man was one of two children, but the only boy in the family. It was obvious to Mac immediately how the parents had clearly doted on their son. He had been due for a week's home leave on the day of the funeral, which seemed to act like a knife cut in the already fragile grief of the family. The dead gunner had had a girlfriend, and she attended the funeral with her parents. Her silence was eerie. She stood, trance-like, for the duration of the service, without a word or a single tear. Mac, mesmerised by her stillness, had never seen a girl quite as pretty, and he felt terrible even thinking it, but there was something deeply disturbing about the depth of her grief which was also beautiful at the same time.

The following day had been hectic too as Mac was required to ensure that various tasks were completed. This included a lot of running around, registering the deceased with the Commonwealth War Graves Commission, arranging for the airman's private possessions to be delivered to Liverpool, and signing the numerous forms for the rail transport services in order to ensure that finances were all settled relating to the transportation of the coffin from the Squadron base. The lengthy list of chores took longer than expected and Mac was still busy on Saturday morning. As a result, he now also had the additional task of liaising with the rail transportation officer in order to extend his 'warrant of duty' so that he might finish the job that he had been assigned.

By the time he was done, Mac felt more than just sympathy for the family he had assisted. He had become close to them as he had soberly liaised with them to carry out his tasks. He made a note to himself that he would write a letter to the family once he was back at base. His mood was low, not improved by a case of the shivers that had begun on Friday evening. By Saturday, his throat was like razorblades and his head was pounding.

His depression was softened by the hospitality of Jean's mother and the unscheduled opportunity to surprise Jean with his presence. Jean's mum declared her intentions to spoil him rotten for a day or two, and Mac was more than happy to submit to her mothering. He spent a couple of days enjoying Jean's company and he felt relaxed and happy when they were together. They were beginning to talk about the prospect of a future together and Mac was sure that Jean was someone with whom he could potentially make a life after the war. Although she was only seventeen years old, he knew that he loved her. Yes, it was far too young to be 'tied down' by a girl, but that was all he could think about. He was beginning to understand why the war brought out an impatience in young couples, a feeling that one should strike while the iron was hot. Tomorrow, just as had happened with the dead gunner whose funeral he had just attended, many men would fail to return from their sorties, so it was little wonder that they were willing to make rash decisions in the pursuit of happiness. Olive, of course, did not share his impatience. Marriage was a serious business and he understood why she would disapprove of him jumping in, feet first. There would, he had assured her, be no quick flights to the altar, but his heart yearned for Jean.

Returning to Wratting Common, refreshed, he found a letter from Olive who advised him that she had finished her job in the ARP and had secured a new position at the Austin. She would be working in the services department, in the tool stores, managing the incoming and outgoing supplies of equipment to the workers on the factory floor. His mother was amazing, indefatigable, and unstoppable. She had taken the hammer-blow of widowhood with steel and worked relentlessly to provide for the four of them, now taking on a job that would wreak havoc with her varicose veins, probably be too heavy and too boring, but he was incredibly proud of her get up and go spirit, and knew that the advantages of more predictable working hours would be helpful for family life.

The RAF continued to keep his mind and body occupied. There was much flying to be done since his return from Liverpool, including a routine flight that was scuppered by fog, necessitating a detour to The Wash in Norfolk, where the crew spent the night. Being an operational base, it provided the boys an invaluable insight into the quality of life they might expect once they joined a squadron. The food was terrific, but the lack of shaving kit and clean clothes made for an uncomfortable and smelly return trip the following day. More exciting was a flight that took them close to the German Buzz Bombers over the south coast of England. Perhaps there was some truth in the adage that you could join the RAF and see the world, after all.

The news from home that Dennis had grown so much that he had taken possession of Mac's overcoat made him realise just how long he had now been away. His smiles at the letter were punctuated by grimaces from the pain in his knee which had been giving him grief since he had fallen off his damn bike that morning. He had been heading to breakfast when a momentary lapse in attention, in the shape of an awfully pretty new WAAF, had been enough to see him plough in to a kerb stone and perform a magnificent nose-dive over the handlebars. The pain had only been overshadowed by the acute embarrassment he had felt, and it would certainly be a while before he lived that one down.

The cold in the hut and the swollen knee he was sporting were not the only things keeping him awake at night for the past day or two either. Considering his state of exhaustion, it was surprising that rest eluded him, but he was now three days overdue in writing to his mother because he was avoiding doing it. What he needed to say in the as yet unwritten letter was troubling him, the proposed contents running circuits around his mind since he had returned from Liverpool. He was frustrated with his own weakness. Although his mother had always encouraged open discussions with Mac about his feelings, this was different. This time he had to talk to her about a decision with which he knew she would disagree. He could almost see her now, wearing a stern expression and crossing her arms at her now-broad, aproned waistline.

He rehearsed a few sentences in his mind before he eventually gave up on sleep altogether. Locating a notepad and the only pencil that had not been 'borrowed' by his roommates, he picked up Olive's most recent letter and turned it in his hands. He could no longer be evasive about the subject of love with either Jean or his mother and he determined to make the necessary declarations to both tonight.

He had made a decision back in Liverpool, and was now determined to execute it. Using the back of Olive's letter to rehearse articulating his feelings, he scrawled a few words from the heart. He transferred the draft into what he hoped was the perfect letter to Jean, then turned his attention to his mum. The sooner he dealt with it, the sooner he could face the consequences and move forward. Even as he wrote, he questioned whether his loyalties to his mother should outweigh his feelings for Jean. Olive was, after all, coping pretty well without his presence at home; there was no reason to think that she would not continue to do so in future. His mother was from strong stock, she was a coper. Life had handed her some ghastly challenges in recent years, but she had never failed to navigate her way through them. The pride he felt for her in this moment softened the edges of his frustration and he suddenly realised that his hesitance over the decision he had made was in large part due to the enormous esteem in which he held her opinion. She mattered a great deal to him and had been his wise guide since he had left school and his father had died. Now he must tread with the utmost care and receive whatever counsel she might offer with grace and gratitude. Feeling like a boy waiting to discover his fate for stealing sweets from a jar, he wrote to his mum to tell her that he was intending to propose marriage to a girl he had met only four months previously. He filled the note with love, flattery, and the respect that he knew she deserved, wishing to assure her of the value that he placed on her counsel and the esteem in which he held her, then he crossed his fingers and waited for the reply.

Olive's response, when it came, was more or less as expected, but with one significant and unexpected positive. She liked Jean. Anxious and uncomfortable about this on his last home leave, the subject of Jean had been the 'elephant in the room', so reading his mother's declaration of approval for his girl of choice was a relief. On the other hand, she was predictably unimpressed about the proposed nuptials, assuming incorrectly that they intended to marry in a hurry, which she rightly considered wholly unnecessary. Mac had no intention of rushing things and neither of them wanted to marry until the war was over. It was impossible for a young couple to plan a future together under the current uncertainties, and he was swift to put Olive's mind at rest on that score.

Olive's life had actually taken a turn for the better in recent weeks as she commenced her new job. While being on her feet all day was taking its toll on her legs, she was enjoying the work very much. It was not too heavy physically but it was interesting and she was starting to get to grips with pulling together orders made up from the 1,001 tools at her disposal, and her foreman was thankfully a gem. Previously taking Saturday mornings off to keep on top of the washing, shopping, and housework, she was now beginning to work weekends too, the opportunity for the extra cash for a fast-approaching Christmas being more tempting than the time at home. Mac had insisted—knowing that she had more than enough to do without the burden of his extra washing parcels—that she stop doing his laundry. Unsurprisingly, Olive refused his offer, her desire to help her son outweighing all of her personal needs.

Her mood was positive and was improved even further when a somewhat impromptu 'breaking up' concert was organised for her old ARP chums. They spent an evening in the Black Horse Pub in Northfield, followed by a shindig at the Grange, where she was plied with ten-year-old homemade parsnip wine. Hardly a drinker, Olive had been tired and somewhat the worse for wear the following day, but her spirits were lifted. News that neighbour Freda's POW husband Norman had also finally returned home safely boosted her further. The end must surely be in sight now.

As fast as Mac could send spare money to Olive, more donations arrived for him from Bank Street, where the locals of the Bridge Inn continued to save their pennies for him. He was grateful, since the Wratting Mess charged bills on a monthly basis and the recent expense of an unfortunate puncture has set him back a gut-wrenching 12/- to put right. Still, he could not be without that bike.

November was whizzing by and 'marking time' at Wratting had become tedious. Relief came on 14th, however, when spaces became available at RAF Feltwell for their final training leg, and the crew moved to Norfolk.

Another midnight arrival, more fatigue, but at least this time they could collapse in a centrally-heated room with a wash basin and hot and cold water. What a pity their stay in such relative luxury was only scheduled to be for ten days.

Soon after their arrival at Feltwell, Harry led his fledgling crew on a long-awaited 'reccy' of their first Lancaster. They were spellbound. It was all they had heard and more, from the neat layout to the home pleasures of the soft armchair, which invited the wireless operator to work in comfort. The attention to detail in the provision of a wrist support was impressive, considering the strain that was placed upon someone who was constantly sending out Morse code. The crew were all desperate to get started on their six days of Ground School and four days of flying that lay ahead.

Flying would be at record altitudes for the crew—23,000, 25,000, 27,000, and ultimately 30,000 feet. Mac knew that the temperatures would be otherworldly up there, at least -40 degrees Centigrade, but spirits were not dampened in the least by the prospect of the cold when they knew it was to be endured within the majesty of the Lancaster. Rear Gunner Ivor had already proven the efficacy of the heated flying suits with which the men had been provided the previous week. Much to the amusement of Mac and his pals, an ill-fated sandwich had been hurriedly shoved into Ivor's pocket before he had promptly forgotten it and taken to the skies. The pleasant aroma of something cooking had alerted him, mid-flight, to the presence of the forgotten sandwich that, once retrieved, had been efficiently toasted for him for lunch.

The crew had sat their 'final, final, final' exams, which all passed comfortably. Ground School was completed, but the much awaited Lancaster flying was disappointingly postponed, so free time was filled with trips to the cinema, sock darning, and letter writing. Once they eventually got up in the beauteous Avro Lancaster, they were not disappointed. Its speed and manoeuvrability impressed the skipper and crew in equal measure, and they could not get enough of her.

Dennis' and Joyce's birthdays came and went, completely passing Mac by, so he sent belated regards. He had been distracted by a horrendous dose of diarrhoea, which had subsided after a couple of days, but he was heartened by the idea of a potential Christmas at home, and the promise of plum puddings for which Olive had declared that she had been saving and scrounging towards for months.

After eleven months of training at eleven different air bases, Mac and crew were finally assigned to a squadron at the end of November 1944. Their new home was 218 Gold Coast Squadron, although they would not transfer directly to their permanent base, instead being diverted to RAF Methwold (remaining in Norfolk) for a short stint of 'special equipment' training, of which he could not speak due to its apparent secrecy. 'Ops' may still be a few weeks away, it seemed.

The distraction of the presence of a long-missed radio in the hut and occasional parcels eased the wait. Jean's packages never disappointed, sending pounds of sweets, apples, *Beano* comics, Brylcreem, soap, and envelopes to keep him fed and supplied. These were topped up by Olive who continued to 'bake and pray' with jam tarts and cakes by mail. The level of jeopardy involved in this exercise had doubled. Mac's continued base-jumping and changes of address made the pies' journeys prolonged and challenging, rarely arriving in one piece, but always eaten with enormous relish.

Methwold was huge, putting a premium on Mac's bike. It was (he had timed it) a full thirty-seven minutes and thirty seconds' walk from their Nissen hut to the Officer's Mess, so he kept it close and treated it as a valued treasure. When the time came to move to their final home at RAF Chedburgh in Suffolk the anticipation was palpable. Mac and his fellow crew were ready, confident, and, most importantly, had absolute faith in each other's abilities to navigate whatever obstacles they might now face, together.

Same place

10·30·p.

Hello Mom,

How's the cold

Hope you have seen the
last of it. I got a letter
from you today, written
last Thursday. I was
very relieved to get
it too. I was going to
write again tonight as it
was. Now I have something
to answer as well.
By the time you got
this you will have
been at Austin's + your
new Job a few days. Don
hope you like it. Well
I say like it; I mean I

hope it isnt to boring
or too hard for you.
That firm isn't exactly
a "heavenly place".
It will be a bind for
you; with the shopping
especially. Are the rates
of pay any better than
the E.P.? I don't want
to know the exact amount
but am just curious?!!
It will be a change for
you to be able to
work to "set" hours
instead of the A.R.P. rota
(If one exists!)
Don't forget to tell me
what you have to do.
By the way, isn't Uncle

Horace in "Service too"?
Now I come to the
difficult part. I have
been trying to pluck
up enough courage to
tell you this for some
weeks past.
Jean and I intend
to get engaged in
the near future.
After she is eighteen
of course.
Do not think too
badly of me. I realise
what I am doing and am
not "going in with my
eyes shut" as you some-
times put it.
We do not intend to

get married till after
the war, so don't think
it will turn out to
be one of the usual
wartime efforts.
Her Dad and Mom are
agreeable but I put
most importance in
your verdict.
Please don't think hard
of me for this Mom, I
have tried to put it to
you as best I can and
if anyone understands
me its you. So you
will know how my
mind is working as I
say this.
Write and let me know

what you think as soon
as possible.
And for my sake please
do not leave this
around where the kid
can mooch at it.
I realise how much
having read this will
have shaken you, but
please look at from
my side too, as I know
you will.
In your letter Denis
asks if he may wear
my best overcoat! Well
I guess so! It will only
go to the moths if he
doesn't wear it!
Wish Joyce the best in

her cookery and tell her
not to try 'em out on
her mates. S'Dangerous.
I was very surprised
to see that Buster
is going in the Para-
troops; still it is his
choice but I'll play safe
and stick to Bomber
Command any day.
Norman Brown has soon
got his wings hasnt
he? It generally take
at least 20 months
to train a pilot, and
then he is only in
the primary stage.
Good-luck to him all
the same. In regards

to writing to Aunt Em
& Co. Well Mom I just
haven't the time. This
is the first letter I
have written to anybody
for 3 days.
We have far to much
to do here to even go
to the pictures and
when we get a day
off (once per 3 weeks) we
are only to glad to
relax.
For all that I will
write "home" as I promise
them. If I am late in
doing so please explain
for me. I may get a
chance tomorrow night

but as you know we've started night flying in these Sterlings and it is a big thing. Well I must finish for tonight as it is late and we are due off the deck at 8 A.M. in the morning. Till the next time Good-night & God-bless

Lots of Love /

Joe +++

9

Virgin Ops

Mac
Raf Chedburgh, Suffolk
4 December 1944–12 December 1944

Chedburgh was a great improvement upon some of the previous places. It was small enough to walk around without transport, and had a good Mess with good grub. Around 6 miles from Bury St Edmunds, the crew could see that they were finally near a town that held treasures, which they could look forward to exploring at a later date. For now, however, life began hard and fast. Olive heard from Mac that the establishment were 'flying the pants off them' and that they had been assigned their own Lancaster—XH-A *A–Able*. It was clear that the men had become quickly attached to the enormous bird which was to be their armour and home for the foreseeable future. She already had one tour under her belt and the crew hoped to add to her provenance with their own stories.

On 11 December, Harry became the first of the crew to taste action as he was assigned as 'second dickie' (observer) to another crew on a daytime raid of Osterfeld, near Essen. Flying alongside Captain George Klenner, the crew gathered together in support and watched him take off on a crisp, cold morning. They were only days in to their Squadron, but were already strangely reluctant to be parted. Nothing was said as his plane disappeared from view, but Harry's absence for those few hours had a big impact on the other six men. The day was full of anxiety, spent in deep thought, each feeling irritable but not fully recognising its cause, and silently willing Harry home safely, feeling nauseous and a little lost without his presence as their leader. Eventually, the sound of engine noise brought the base back to life as everyone scurried to meet the returning crew buses. Rushing bodies headed for the briefing room where they were met by the ever-smiling face of their skipper who said, 'Hello boys. It's a piece of cake!'

The uneventful nature of Harry's virgin trip had served to break his duck and relieve the tension, but would also put Harry on a firm footing for what was to come the following day with their first 'Op'.

On 12 December, the crew awoke at 7.20 a.m., shaved stubbly chins in the regular dating ritual which a chin required when meeting an oxygen mask, yanked on Long Johns, and tried to steady nervous hands by turning attention to the necessary multiple layers of clothing for the pending cold. Vests were followed by shirts and pullovers, battledress trousers, electric Sidcot suits, and fur-lined boots and coats. As the 'new boys', the crew were conscious of their own lack of chatter as they enjoyed a pre-flight breakfast of bacon and eggs. The noise elsewhere was reassuring—laughter and banter echoed in the Mess, but as they converged on the briefing room for details of their first 'Op' their confidence was high. Although not arrogant, the seven men were young and brash, and felt self-assured and well-disciplined. They felt as though they were the best crew in the business with their straight-shooting gunners, Mac and Ivor, and accurate bomber, Bill. Ivor had noted that 'Alec could navigate them through a rice pudding, Tom could engineer their flying back on a tube of lighter fuel, and Harry could fly anything, anywhere, anytime'.

The long tables of the briefing room were already crowded with navigators poring over maps, drawing lines, and conferring with pilots and engineers who were studying charts. At the far end of the long hut was a small stage where a large map of Germany was positioned. Red tape ran from an equally red pin in England (indicating Chedburgh) to other red pins in Germany. They looped around and back again, indicating the return route home. Mac was excited, but strangely unafraid, as the roll-call commenced.

The target was to be Witten. Intelligence Officers detailed how they were to bomb an oil and coking plant at the far end of the 'Happy' (Ruhr) Valley. A virgin target for a virgin crew, they were headed for a busy plant that needed to be taken out of production. The Met men gave a weather briefing—cloud over 4–5 tenths, thickening to 5–8 tenths in the south; visibility 3 miles; ice and where to expect it.

Once the briefing was over, there was a sense of relief. There was no more uncertainty and Mac and his fantastic crew-mates knew their jobs well enough. They collected their parachutes and the rest of their flying gear from their lockers, assembling electric gloves and gauntlets, helmets, and Mae Wests together. Mac wrapped his 'wakey-wakey' pills in a twist of paper and stuffed them in a pocket before methodically checking his equipment. The checklist took his mind off their scheduled flying time of 10.30 a.m., and he mentally ticked off CO_2 bottles, escape kits, floating lamps, and sweets until he noted the time as 9.15 a.m. and headed with his pals for the crew bus.

CHED.

Monday.

Hello Mom,

Well I'm just going to drop you a short note to let you know I'm o.k.

Harry went over Germany on a raid today to Osterfeld nea Essen. We did not go, just him thats all! He acted as second "dickie" (pilot) to some other crew.

We are on ops tomorrow but I can't say yet where. I will write & tell you what I can about it in tomorrow after we've got back.

Well I said this was to be a short letter and so it is!

That is about all the

news at present or till
tomorrow God-bless +
"Olive Oil,"

lots
of love

+ + +
+ + +
+ + + +
+ + +
+ + +

Roll on Xmas and
leave (I hope!!)

I want to get some
Xmas-pudding-eating-
-hours in !!

10

A Ditching

Olive
Northfield, Birmingham
12 December 1944–23 December 1944

The last letter Olive had received from Joe had been written on Monday 11 December. Joe had said that he would be on his first operation the following day, but by Saturday, Olive had yet to hear from her son. She was anxious and irritable. He rarely went four days without writing home, and her mind was playing terrible tricks on her. She cursed his thoughtlessness for not writing to reassure her; surely he must understand how on edge the family would be, knowing that he was on his first sortie?

Olive spent that Saturday morning at work, continuing to cram in the overtime to try to subsidise the family's Christmas budget. Her mind was on Joe but she distracted herself with thoughts of the endless list of jobs she needed to do around the house. She still had to get the ironing finished, the shopping done, the fowl killed, and the kids fed and in bed before she could sit down and write to her eldest again.

By the time she returned home, she was already exhausted. Her sore legs served as a constant reminder that she needed to visit the doctor about her veins. As she was pondering this, there was a knock at the front door. The next thing she heard was Joyce screaming. Olive rushed through from the kitchen at the back of the house, intent on giving her daughter a piece of her mind for the intolerable racket she was making. All was forgotten in an instant, however, as she saw Joyce wrapped around the waist of the tall figure of Joe, standing large as life in her front room with a peculiarly neon yellow face and a beaming smile.

It turned out that Joe had beaten his own overdue letter home. The yellow face was not as a result of jaundice, as his mother had at first suspected, but had been caused by a much more serious incident that had led to Mac's sudden appearance at home on emergency leave. Furnished with a cup of tea, he set about recounting the events that had led to his unexpected arrival.

As they had left on the crew bus and moved out to the perimeter track on that morning of 12 December, they had each felt a sense that they were doing good, but could not help wondering about the statistics. Getting the 'chop' was a serious possibility after all. Joe remembered gathering his kit when he heard their call, no longer for *A-Able*, but for new 'kite' *C-Charlie* and jumping off the bus. *C-Charlie* was standing with bomb doors open and looking formidable as they boarded her. They ran through their pre-flight check lists. Guns, ammunition, oxygen points, turrets, tyres, flaps, wings—it was a well-known routine, but it felt good to be busy, especially on this first morning. They left the aircraft for a final breather before Harry had declared it time to go. Olive and the kids laughed as Mac, enjoying the audience, demonstrated how he had knelt on the ground at that point and kissed it. Slapping the tarmac affectionately he wished it 'ta-ta' and told it he would be back.

Joe had wormed his way into his turret and the engines had started one by one. It was quite a feat just getting into position for the crew in their flying gear, and they often arrived out of breath before they had even left the ground. As they moved past the briefing room, the plane rattled and shook. Joe's turret did the same, and him with it. They could see crowds of bodies outside waiting to watch the Lancasters disperse and each of the observers gave the 'V' signal as the departing crews passed by.

Some while after take-off, they had located *Q-Queenie*, their formation leader, and followed her with little chat for some time. The monotony of flight was occasionally interrupted for Joe by debilitating cramp or the need to remove icicles from the valve of his oxygen mask. Ivor watched the stream of aircraft that tailed behind them from his rear position. He reported that a couple of kites turned back, but otherwise all was quiet.

The cold was intense. Joe had plugged in his electric suit, but this served only to take the edge off the cold and prevent hypothermia or frostbite at 20,000 feet. The draught was biting in the turret and he was, as always, desperate to stretch his legs, feeling irritable with the lack of space and the itchy oxygen mask that he would not be able to remove for several hours yet.

They had seen their first flak as they crossed the French coast. Mac told the kids how pretty it had looked, clouds like little white and black balloons hanging in the air. They had reached their planned rendezvous point with the fighter escorts and Joe and Ivor had scoured the skies for them without success. Tom had followed the skipper's instructions to release bundles of 'window' at two-minute intervals. Since Mac and crew were in the leading group of aircraft, they took little comfort from the intended objective of the 'window', which was to jam enemy radar and prevent detection, since there were no shimmering pieces of foil floating past their own aircraft.

Eventually, a group of fighters were spotted off the port side, too far away to identify with certainty. Within seconds, the gunners had realised that they were looking at enemy Me 109s. As they spotted a brown plummet of smoke snaking down the whirling column of small fighter planes, they realised that their first attack was about to begin. There was too much adrenaline and activity for fear. Harry talked calmly over the intercom and prepared the crew to fight it out.

The chaos began very suddenly. A Lancaster below them was corkscrewing and flames were visible on her port wing. The smoke thickened and bits began to fall off the aircraft, which ceased returning fire and fell into a slow spiral downwards. Then there was another Lancaster in smoke, fighters coming from so many directions that Joe and Ivor could not keep up with them. The two gunners tried to watch them all, in the hope of working out where an attack would come from; their minds were racing. Parachutes were here and there and their hearts were in their mouths.

The loud noise of an explosion deafened the crew and the skipper reassured them that he had *C-Charlie* under control. They were flying in flak. Panic was only held at bay by the need to deal with an Me 109 that was lining up for an attack on the port bow. A second explosion made *C-Charlie* suddenly jump, followed by shaking and shuddering, and there was the sound of tearing metal. Ivor noticed that smoke was trailing from the port wing as he managed to line up his sights on the Me 109. The next thing Mac heard was Ivor's panicked voice declaring that his oxygen had run out.

Joe Naisbitt was dispatched hurriedly to assist Ivor, who had passed out. Joe managed to manhandle Ivor to the Elsan Closet at the rear of the plane and reconnected his oxygen tube.

As Joe narrated the story, Brian's eyes grew wider and wider as he elaborated on the action. Olive was speechless, struggling to comprehend the severity of what her son was describing. While all this madness was going on in the aircraft, he continued, they had finally managed to see off their attack but were limping badly. They had reached the target and Bill had effectively sent away the payload. By the time the bombs were away, they had lost the port outer engine, but Harry declared that the aircraft was manageable, despite the fact that they were losing fuel. They were at least now heading home.

Ivor had been out long enough to completely miss all of the fun, but finally came around with a big thumbs up. He got up and tried to crawl back to his turret, stretching the oxygen pipe as far as it would go. He could not reach the turret but could get far enough to see that it was devastated. There was no bottom to it, no Perspex, and jagged chunks of fuselage curled in from the tail unit. Oil was everywhere from the broken servo pipes, so Ivor crawled back to the Elsan closet and put his head in his hands, feeling unusually useless.

Tom and Harry discussed their options with haste. They were losing fuel at too fast a rate to make it back home by following the rest of the stream. Alec was ordered to plot the straightest route to base and the skipper turned *C-Charlie* away from the relative safety of flying with company on to an unescorted route home, knowing that they had sustained too much damage to take the usual route and would have to go it alone.

Joe's heart jumped as he spotted a fighter to starboard and relaxed just as quickly when he realised it was one of theirs. The Mustang pilot pulled alongside the Lancaster and gave the crew the thumbs up. Minutes later, a sudden vibration was followed by Harry's voice on the intercom, indicating that they had now also lost the port inner engine. Mac could tell they were losing height and speed (they were now at 14,000 feet) but the skipper, calm as ever, reassured them that they were OK. Tom sounded less sure that they would make it—the fuel was running out faster and they were getting seriously low. With their position confirmed as somewhere over the Zuiderzee in Holland, it became clear that Tom was right. There was a splutter and a dip and Harry relayed the bad news to the crew that they were losing the starboard inner engine too.

Harry asked the boys what they wanted to do: bale out or stay with the aeroplane and hope to get to the North Sea before they ditched her? It was an easy decision. They wanted to stay together with their crew and their kite. Besides, no one fancied baling out into the Zuiderzee.

Joe Naisbitt sent out the emergency signals when they were at 8,000 feet. They would be over the sea in about fifteen minutes, but close to the Dutch coast. The skipper agreed to call out the altitude as they went down. There was such a calmness about him that the boys felt relieved to have such a pilot at their controls, yet at the same time curiously concerned that he seemed to be enjoying it.

Mac took a deep breath and steeled himself before sliding down from his turret and jettisoning the overhead escape hatch. Bill had squeezed through the fuselage doorway and climbed into his ditching position on the bunk. Mac and Ivor lay on the floor, which formed the top of the bomb bay, their feet pressed into the flapjack funnel to stop them sliding forward. Mac had no intercom point to plug in to, so from this moment on would have to rely on signals from Ivor. His voice caught as he told Olive how he had felt isolated and scared until he had felt Ivor's arm go around his shoulder, receiving a quick squeeze. Mac stared at Ivor, who had lifted the ear flap of his helmet and shouted over the engine noise that he would squeeze him again when it was time to brace, and that he would try to indicate height by counting with his fingers.

For the next few minutes they listened to the sound of Harry's heavy breathing as he battled with the kite. Their lives now in his hands, their trust held strong, this situation serving only to elevate him in their esteem. The engine stopped and spluttered back to life a number of times as they dipped forward and backward. Responding to Harry's voice, Ivor raised four fingers to indicate 4,000 feet, then a few seconds later, three. Almost immediately after that, Ivor raised just one finger. Joe's puzzled face must have said it all—what happened to two? They were hitting hard and fast. Then came the squeeze, followed by an enormous impact and tremendous vibration. There was a sudden surge of water and Joe was on his feet immediately, apparently and unexpectedly intact. Speed was now of the essence and the distant recollection of tedious dinghy drills in the sea at Bridlington front of mind. The floor was moving up and down—the first indication that they were afloat and they speedily reached for the cord for the emergency dinghy release. It came away hand over hand, having obviously become detached from the dinghy on impact. A glance to the rear of the trashed plane brought a shock as it had severed in two and the remains of Ivor's turret now appeared to be floating away with the tail-plane.

Mac indicated with a movement of the head that they should use the escape hatch and they struggled out in their bulky gear, pushing and shoving each other to speed things up. It was clear that *C-Charlie* would not be floating for much longer. Alec, Tom, and Joe N. were already out on the starboard wing. As Mac and Ivor sat on top of the fuselage, they turned to see Harry pulling clear of another hatch that had been above his head. This was a moment that they would never forget. Mac laughed now as he told Olive about Harry's reaction upon emerging. For a moment he had sat on the edge on top of the cockpit canopy with his back to the rest of the crew. As he had pulled his legs clear he looked round, grinning. 'Well boys, we made it,' he had shouted, with a look of triumph. They had never doubted the skipper's ability to bring them down safely, but they knew there was a long way to go before they were in the clear.

With one awful story following another, Olive grimaced as Mac explained how none of the dinghy release mechanisms had worked. Joe Naisbitt had moved towards the Perspex panel on the wing, which housed one of them, and kicked it several times with his flying boot until it smashed. Alec reached in with his arm, pulled out the dinghy and it burst into life with a bang and a hiss. At that moment, a wave broke over the wing and swept both Alec and the dinghy into the water, causing Mac to swear in shock. The dinghy was supposed to be tethered to the aircraft so that it could not be washed away, but Alec was clearly struggling to keep his head above water and hold on to it. Ivor jumped without hesitation straight in to the icy water to help pull the dinghy toward the rest of the crew on the fuselage. He was the strongest swimmer, but the weight of his clothes was preventing him reaching them. The realisation that they would now have to swim to the dinghy in the icy December waters in full gear was sobering. One at a time, they jumped and swam, clumsily and frustratingly slowly to the dinghy where they hauled one another, freezing cold and exhausted into the inflated vessel, over the high waves that they had drunk by the bucketful. Once aboard, they hauled in the ration boxes, which dangled around the side of the dinghy, attached by cords.

Alec's finger was bleeding profusely from his battle with the dinghy and a large chunk of flesh appeared to be hanging by a thread. Harry bandaged him clumsily and they paddled away from the fuselage. Alec produced a crumpled and damp map from his pocket and proceeded to estimate their position as roughly halfway between England and Holland, having ditched at approximately 3.20 p.m. They became aware of an engine sound above them. Their faithful escort had located them and was hopefully alerting the rescue crews of their position.

Hypothermia was now a big risk. Bill looked awful, shivering and becoming violently seasick. They set up the weather apron, which provided a full canopy to shelter from the spray and wind, expecting that it could be the following day before they were picked up. They bailed out the water, which was swirling around their feet, and were half grateful when the seasickness emptied their stomachs of the potent yellow die that they had ingested with the sea water they had swallowed. This, Mac explained to Olive, was the reason for his current neon-canary complexion, which was still present four days later. He explained how the sea dye was dispersed around the dinghy in order to assist the search and rescue crews in locating them in the vast darkness of the ocean. Brian and Joyce had stopped giggling about Joe's yellow face a while ago, such was the tension over his story.

He told them how their escort had flown over them low, waving his wings. They took it to be a goodbye signal, presumably fuel low and heading home. During the next hour, they had watched the fuselage of *C-Charlie* slowly sinking. There was an air of melancholy and pride in their aircraft, which had stood up well to such a pounding. They would be sorry to lose her.

After a while, a Walrus seaplane finally appeared and the crews' hopes rose, until they realised that it would be impossible for it to land in the large swells that surrounded them. Joe N. watched carefully as a winking light relayed the message that their position had been transmitted to the ASR (Air Sea Rescue) boys. They dropped a black object in to the water near to the dinghy, from which smoke rose upwards. It was a smoke float, designed to give a more definite idea of their direction of drift, in order to maximise the ASR crew's chance of locating the dinghy.

Eventually, the Walrus left and the light began to fade. The crew took turns watching and listening for help, with only heads protruding from the weather canopy. No one really spoke. The retching got so bad that they found it hard not to think about dying, such was their misery in the cold and wet. Harry had been firing flares at intervals, and as night began to close in, they agreed to fire one every hour throughout the night.

Around three hours passed, and every now and then, they poked their heads out to watch and ease the monotony. Then, out of the corner of his eye, Alec spotted what seemed to be a light. It moved closer and it eventually became clear that it was a Navy destroyer. The excitement was palpable and the crew waved and cheered like children as it approached, acknowledging their presence. Harry requested calm and reminded them that they were, after all, RAF gentlemen.

Boarding the ship was challenging in the extreme. The swell had risen to about 12 feet and the dinghy sloshed about, rising up and down so that it was sometimes level with the deck of the ship, and then suddenly falling away again. This made it impossible to make the leap, especially from an unsteady dinghy where they were struggling to stand. Eventually, the captain of the ship instructed his men to clip a deck ladder to the ship's side. The boys were told to attempt get a foot on the ladder each time the swell lifted the dinghy to rise level with it, and then to hold fast and allow the dinghy to fall away. The ship's crew would grab hold of each of them and haul them on board. One by one, Tom, Joe, Bill, Mac, Alec, Ivor, and finally Harry slowly made it from raft to ship. This was treacherous, precarious work and almost as terrifying as the ditching itself.

They were each hurried below decks where, with the assistance of others, they laboriously stripped off their wet gear. They towelled themselves dry, drank cocoa, and smoked the cigarettes that were offered by their rescuers.

It was soon clear that the ship that had actually found them had not been their intended rescue vessel at all. The ship had actually been returning from a routine patrol and had spotted the flair signal by accident. The crew had drifted in the dinghy such a long way from the position that the Mustang escort had provided that ASR had been searching the wrong area, eventually giving up looking for them due to the rough seas and poor visibility. They were doubly lucky to be alive.

They had made it eventually back to Chedburgh where sleep and food had revived them and lifted their spirits. Mac had written to Olive and Jean to tell them both not to worry, but he had arrived before his own letter.

This would have been a disastrous outing for any crew, but for it to happen on their first mission was truly unfortunate. Olive thought about Harry Warwick, the captain of this band of men who had dutifully kept them safe. She owed him an enormous debt of gratitude. He would no doubt be preoccupied with the job he now had to do in order to regroup his crew and raise their confidence before the Ops began again.

Olive and the children listened intently to this story again and again over the next seven days of Mac's leave. As his yellow face faded, his retelling of the story took on a lighter touch, customarily laughing it off as nothing of significance, but doing little to relieve his mother of the permanent knot she would feel in her stomach for some time to come.

Mac had rarely appreciated the comforts of home as he did on this occasion and Olive was in no hurry to have him leave so close to Christmas. The smells, sights, and sounds of festivities were in the air in Northfield, making it all the more difficult to think about the fact that his leave period would soon be over and he would once more be in jeopardy. She hoped and prayed that his home stay might be extended up to and beyond the new year, but that was not to be.

(P.S.
I may beat this letter home!)

CHED
Thursday

Hello Mom,

First of all, excuse the writing material, I'm in a hell of a rush!! I'm coming home in a day or so on survivors leave! We were shot up over ~~Germany~~ on our first op and crashed in the North Sea. We we picked up after 3 hours. We all got out O.K. and are well. Try and imagine swimming in the North Sea in December?!! Cold aint it?!! We slept 14 hours after being picked up...!! I'm alright so don't worry Mom...It looks as if I will get Xmas at home after all, at least I hope so.! God-bless & See you soon.

Lots of Love Joe

x x x
x x x
x x x

11

A Marriage, a Death, and a Lot of Near Misses

Mac
RAF Chedburgh, Suffolk
23 December 1944–31 March 1945

After seven days' emergency leave, the crew were recalled to Chedburgh. It was the day before Christmas Eve and the journey had been a nightmare. The train from Birmingham New Street to Euston had been delayed by over five hours, and Mac arrived back at the RAF station at 9.30 a.m. Two hours later, they were called out flying, being sent to Mildenhall to collect a new plane. There would be no rest for the festive season.

Mac had left Olive and Jean at the train station, feeling dreadful. His insides had felt as though they were tied in a knot and he had been more than a little reluctant to let them go. His engagement with Jean had become official some time ago and he was frustrated by the need to return so soon. On the news of Joe's ditching, Jean had immediately come to Birmingham for a visit, worried sick about Joe and desperate to hear his stories, so Olive had invited her to stay for Christmas, assuming incorrectly that Joe would still be home. Love and the comfort of his mother's cooking had been a serious tonic for him following the trauma of the preceding days, and he was already feeling homesick and nervous at the thought of what lay ahead. Despite his attempts to laugh off his near-death experience with his theatrical minute by minute retelling of it, the event had seriously impacted Mac and he had relished his time at home recuperating.

His first op after returning was scheduled for Christmas Day, but was scrubbed at the last minute, allowing Joe and the boys the chance to eat a hearty Mess Christmas dinner, complete with turkey, chicken, plum pudding, nuts, oranges, mince pies, and apples. He would, of course, have given all of that up for a chance to be sitting around Olive's table, and the thought of it had put a damper on the festivities around the base. The entire crew was feeling the same, so the two Joes and Tom had all opted out of the evening's planned dance and booze-up in the Mess as they nursed a similarly 'cheesed off' frame of mind.

Christmas came to them in the form of news and parcels from home. Jean's mother sent Mac a Christmas cake and there was a luxurious beaver bristle shaving brush from

Jean. News of how the celebrations back home were going left Joe with mixed feelings, but he revelled in the stories of Jean mixing with his relatives and thought that it boded well for their future together. The Woodcock clan, Olive's sisters, and their respective husbands often played host at Christmas, and it was always lively. Mac had been anxious about whether the shy Jean would fit in with the rather more rowdy elements of his family, and hoped that they would all like each other. He really need not have worried on that score, it seemed. In fact, Jean had been enjoying such a time that she had stayed on for an extra few days, only leaving when her mother had sent a telegram from Liverpool. He still allowed himself a small chuckle at his mother's description of his three raucous uncles apparently putting in some excellent work under the mistletoe with his girl. It was a wonder poor Jean did not go home with foot-and-mouth disease.

The next few days were full of flying, but no ops. The crew were declared fit for full duties again by 29 December, and by New Year's Eve, they would be back at it.

During that week, dark news had reached Mac of the loss of two Canadians, including close pal Kilty who had so often sent his laundry home to Olive. The news of his loss hit Joe hard as Kilty had been the most excellent chap. This, he realised, was now his new reality. His friends were in mortal danger each and every time they took to the sky, and for the sake of the people who relied so heavily upon him, he must stay safe. The odds suggested that this was an impossible dream, and his doubts were made worse by the loss of a second friend from Chedburgh in the very same week.

It seemed a lifetime since their first op had ended in such disaster, and they were more than a little nervous when they were woken early on New Year's Eve and briefed for a daylight attack on Vohwinkel in the Ruhr Valley. The target was to be the Railway Marshalling Yard, where freight trains were changed and stored. Among the crews flying that day were those led by the Australian pilot Klenner, Bates, Wilson, Hill, Mears, and the New Zealander McClennan. Harry Warwick and co. took off at 11.26 a.m. toward the rear of the group.

All crews dropped their bombs on the target, but the bombing was not concentrated due to the ragged formation of the squadron. Harry's crew struggled to find leaders or followers in the 10/10 cloud cover and strong winds, and the weather played a part in two subsequent incidents, which occurred as the crews completed their mission. While they watched one cookie blow up in the stream beneath a follower aircraft, miraculously leaving the aircraft and crew unhurt, Mac's crew had a closer-than-close engagement with a fellow Lancaster. Somehow, as they were crossing out over the English Channel, a second Lancaster nosed up into the belly of their aircraft, *B-Baker*, colliding with them in mid-air. An almighty bump could be heard and it threw the seven men back into their seats. Their bomb bay doors were smashed and the port tail plane was also damaged. A quick assessment of the damage left Harry feeling confident that they were OK, and they managed to complete the bombing mission, escaping in one piece and this time managing to avoid the watery depths of the North Sea. They returned to base after a little more than five hours in the air. Mac was relieved to be on *terra firma* once more.

On New Year's Day, they were off to Vohwinkel again, but this time on their first major night operation in *D-Dog*. Mac hated it. The penetrating darkness made it almost impossible to see whether they were close to other aircraft. Mac knew that his role in the aircraft as a gunner was to continuously observe. From the moment their wheels left the ground until they were back down again, he would have to scout the black skies for enemy aircraft, which might come from any of the 360-degree directions he could see. It was an exhausting first experience in the black of a winter's night and he felt the pressure.

Fifteen aircraft left in poor visibility, but by the time they approached the target, the weather cleared a little, enough for them to make visual contact with Vohwinkel. By around 7 p.m., the crew were in the heart of the action and found themselves picked out for attack by an enemy fighter. A Dornier 217 approached them from the side. Mac happened to spot the attack first so, with adrenaline pumping, he shouted 'here we go again' and gave him a 'squirt'. The fighter passed into Ivor's rear turret zone and was welcomed with another fifty rounds of .303, after which time the guns of Ivor's rear turret, suddenly and inopportunely, completely packed up. This was clearly more than a little inconvenient, and Ivor found that his ammunition had begun to run free through the bottom entry ducts, piling up in the base of his turret and trapping his legs completely. Joe continued to work to see off the fighter as best he could, unaware of the extent of Ivor's strife. The mayhem in the rear turret had now also managed to cut off all Ivor's intercom leads, rendering him unable to communicate with the rest of the crew successfully. Thankfully, the attack failed to make its mark upon their aircraft, but it was hard to say whether Mac or Ivor had made a reciprocal mark on the Dornier either. The drama continued when they were hit by a cannon shell on the port fin a few minutes later, then narrowly missed a collision with another Lancaster on the starboard side. The crew were rattled but thankfully completely unscathed as they bombed the target and proceeded to set off for home. After six hours and forty-five minutes in the air, poor weather conditions welcomed them, forcing a diversion to RAF Dishforth, near Ripon in North Yorkshire. The diversion gave them time to reflect on their experiences to date. Was every op going to be like this? It was real seat-of-the-pants stuff. There was little doubt about that, in spite of the false sense of security into which Harry's first 'second dickie' op had lured them.

Olive received the news that the crew had returned to the skies of Germany, in the bitter cold of this new year, with trepidation. Each and every letter from her son filled her heart with gratitude that her nightly prayers were being answered. While ever the envelopes kept arriving with his handwriting on, she knew all was well. Mac's attempts to show her that his spirits were strong did not necessarily fool her, and his recurring closing line, 'Keep smiling, I do', did not remove her ever-present worry.

Mac had caught a cold as soon as he was back on ops, but in spite of this, he and the boys were starting to feel strangely invincible. They had managed to negotiate the perils of a handful of hair-raising ops whose content had been enough to finish off many a crew that had gone before them, and yet they were all unharmed and still upbeat.

On 7 January, they were briefed for a very hot target: Munich. They were aiming for the old residential part of the city on an 'obliteration' raid. It was a long night flight, the longest yet by far. With 2,000 gallons of fuel on board aircraft *A-Apple*, their bombload had to be reduced to 4½ tons as they were unable to carry any further weight. It was a 1,700-mile trip and would require Mac to sit in one uncomfortable position, intently focusing on the skies around him, for eight hours and ten minutes. Some very serious fighter opposition kept Mac and Ivor extremely busy dealing with the barrage of attacks. They had endured a long, frantic, and tense journey of stiff German defences, being greeted at the target by a considerable force of Ju 88s, which had been sent to intercept the stream. Intense anti-aircraft fire, heavy searchlights, and bitter cold all added to their discomfort, and Mac witnessed at least three other aircraft had exploded before they had released their bombs. Shaken, but unscathed, they set off for home, only to be caught in a predicted flak attack over Stuttgart. While they were not hit, the blast from a near miss was so violent and close that Ivor in the rear turret was knocked unconscious again. Harry nosed down at 290 mph, diving them skilfully away from the offending area while the boys attended to Ivor who was again, by some miracle, unhurt. They landed safely at Chedburgh, exhausted. By the end of the extensive operation, their nerves were like torn rags, but they were able to claim two destroyed enemy aircraft as well as a further two 'probables'.

Further ops came, including a Krefeld-Uerdingen sortie that ended in an early return to base, having not bombed. The sorties were punctuated by days of grounding or training flights here and there and they entertained themselves between ops with trips to the cinema. *Phantom of the Opera, Dragon Seed, Song of Russia*, all serving their purpose of taking their minds off the next day's events.

Op number 6 was a daylight raid on the Marshalling Yards at Saarbrücken. This was a huge, 1,000 bomber raid and the boys were in *D-Dog*. They left base early on Saturday 13 January and completed their op safely and without incident. On the route home, however, they were instructed by radio to land at St Eval in Cornwall. The extra 230 miles on their journey did nothing for their spirits and tempers were frayed. The overnight stay at St Eval would have been a welcome rest, but a 2 a.m. start on 15 January put paid to that as a raid on Erkenswick's coking plant was scheduled.

All went well for once, and relief came in the form of some well-earned leave at the end of January. It was to be a big one for skipper, Harry, who had planned that this would be the leave when he would be married to his fiancée. The boys wished him well and parted in high spirits, knowing that the old man would return to them as, if it were at all possible, even more of a patriarchal figure than the one who left.

Mac headed to Liverpool, where his own fiancée was busy filling her bottom drawer with all manner of 'surprises'. As ever, the trains proved challenging, and Mac's predicted 12 p.m. arrival turned into a nine-and-a-half-hour delay. By the time he actually arrived at Lime Street Station, Jean had made a total of three unsuccessful visits there to meet him. Her anxiety had been clear to see, and Jean had mobbed him when they finally caught up with each other. Jean's mother's set-aside dinner had eventually been pronounced extinct and had been discarded. Mac made himself immediately at home, waking the following morning to tea and toast in bed, and then sleeping like a king until midday.

A trip over to Hoylake was planned, in order to visit Joe Naisbitt and his intended, Barbara, and an evening at the Pantomime in the company of Albert Wheelan and Colinson & Brean provided light entertainment before he had to head back to Bury St Edmunds and night ops. Joe N.'s presence provided welcome company on the parched, hungry, delayed twelve-hour trip back to base.

Mac had now clocked up over 200 hours of flying in his logbook. It was frustrating to watch other crews ending their tours with less hours in their logbooks than he had already flown, but there was little he could do about that.

By the end of January, Chedburgh base had clocked up 150 day-time and seventy night raids during the month, almost 1,000 hours of flying in total among the crews stationed there. A total of 782 tons of bombs had been dropped and three DFCs awarded as a result of the encounters they had dealt with.

February would be busier still for the base, and Mac and crew were back on duty and right in the thick of it by the 3rd. A Saturday night flight, they boarded *E-Edmund* for the target: Dortmund. This was another 'obliteration' raid on the city, as well as an intended attack on the Hansa Coking Plant. Grateful that they were not scheduled to return to Munich, Mac and crew assumed that anything else would be a breeze. They were quite wrong. It turned out to be by far the worst of their sorties so far, the whole of the Ruhr Valley alive with battles, fires, and searchlights. Finding themselves in the midst of severe opposition coming from all quarters, Mac and crew were then 'coned' by searchlights, from which only the skipper's excellent skills freed them. Having eluded one drama, they then found themselves in the grip of five separate 'Heavies' cannon attacks. It was a night of very close shaves and rattled nerves. Once grounded, however, pride quickly outweighed fear as Harry's crew discovered the accuracy of their bombing, when in-flight photographs revealed that they had the most effective bombing results of the whole squadron.

Mac was still recovering from this most recent nerve-racking outing when rumours arose that a standard tour was to be extended from thirty to thirty-five, or even forty, ops. With their experience so far and the targets appearing to be getting harder, the prospect of entering the fray for a considerably longer period was not welcome news. With any luck, the Russians would have the job finished before it came to that.

The prospect of a presentation to the crew of their 'Goldfish' award threw Mac into a wobble. He loathed being the centre of attention at the best of times, so the idea of a parade that celebrated the crew's successful December 'ditching', with him at the centre, was an unwelcome one. He would just stay away, he decided.

The day after the Dortmund sortie, all thoughts of Goldfish, ops, or pretty much anything else vanished, when tragedy struck out of nowhere. On 4 February, standing down from ops for a brief respite, some of the boys had made the most of the time off with trips into town for a little R&R. Mac's friend and the crew's bomb aimer, Bill Perry, had been among those choosing to venture into Bury St Edmunds. As was traditional after a night out, he had congregated outside the railway station to await the RAF transport truck that transferred the men back to Chedburgh. He and others climbed over the tailgate and sat in the rear of the truck for the journey back to the station. At around 11 p.m., the truck approached the entrance to the base, but the driver found himself partially blinded by the lights of an oncoming vehicle, so pulled over to the side of the road to let it pass. Believing the truck to have stopped for passengers to alight, Bill had vaulted the tailgate of the vehicle on to the road. In one tragic and horrific moment, the truck driver, realising that he had overshot the entrance to the station, reversed the enormous vehicle directly over Bill, killing him instantly. He was just twenty-two years old.

When the news reached Mac, Harry, *et al.* towards midnight, disbelief and devastation set in. Bill was a very well loved and popular crewmember and a first-class bomber. He had joined the RAF in April 1942 and had trained in Canada before receiving a commission in December 1943. He was the middle of three sons, and his older brother, Don, was already famous as he played football for Cheltenham Town and was a cricketer for Gloucestershire CCC. Don was now serving as a captain in the Gurkhas. Bill's younger brother, Stuart, was in the Royal Navy, making a full military complement for the family.

Several days of sober mourning followed, before the sombre and very well-attended funeral for Bill took place at St Mary's Church in his hometown of Charlton Kings on Monday 12 February. Knowing that it would be unlikely that Bill's own two brothers would be able to get to the funeral, it became imperative to Harry and the remaining crewmembers that they should all attend to represent the squadron. They acted as escort for their friend on this one last outing together, and Mac was moved to tears by the deep respect and esteem in which Bill and his family were held not only by his fellow RAF crewmen, but also clearly by their local community.

An inquest was held in the days between the death and the funeral in Bury, under Coroner Thomas Wilson. A WAAF who had been travelling on the same truck, seated next to the driver, provided a witness statement that corroborated the fact that the driver had been entirely unaware that the young airman had exited the vehicle and had reversed in order to be as close as possible to the entrance to the base, killing Bill in an instant. A verdict of 'misadventure' was concluded, doing little to alleviate the terrible grief and stress for either the family, or the truck driver, but nonetheless providing confirmation that it had indeed been a terrible and tragic accident.

Bill was sorely missed, and the crew stood down from ops for two weeks.

The short respite from flying came to an end with a sortie to Chemnitz on Valentine's Day. Seventeen aircraft left, but Mac's crew never got there, thanks to the loss of an engine before they had even crossed the battle line in the south of France. As well as the missing Bill, the trip had been made without navigator Alec, who was in hospital suffering with hellishly painful sinus problems. It had been so acute during flight that Alec had fainted on the way back from their Dortmund outing a couple of weeks prior. Ivor was also struggling, this time with an ear infection, so he too was grounded for a few days to recover. Mac's confidence was not the same without them all, but thankfully this was an easy trip.

Leave was due on 8 March, and Mac was desperate to see Jean again, so invited her to join him at home in Birmingham. Disappointment came when the leave was deferred for a further two weeks, however, and Mac was irritated beyond belief. Jean had taken the week of the 8th off work, and this bad news, although technically only a small setback, sent his spirits hurtling downwards. The temporary decimation of his crew, the loss of Bill, and his desperation to be home with his family and Jean were depressing and demoralising blows. He tried to lift his low mood but was finding it incredibly difficult to do so.

A few days later, on Sunday, the afternoon was spent on a daylight raid to Wesel. It proved straightforward in *B-Baker*, since the opposition was moderate but erratic, resulting in the destruction of the whole town. Bad weather again forced a landing at an alternative aerodrome, where they were forced to stay overnight.

Daytime sleep was grabbed where it could be had, in readiness for the regular night-time raids that had become standard, although the fact that they were increasingly mixed with daylight trips was making sleep difficult to achieve.

They were scheduled for a return to Dortmund a few days later, but had to abort in *A-Apple* after unlucky Ivor's electric heater suit caught fire. After almost three hours in the air, his right arm began to spontaneously combust, causing him surface burns and forcing the crew to return to base.

On 22 February, Gelsenkirchen provided another nasty experience. A cloudless sky meant that the fourteen aircraft that were despatched encountered deadly flak both on the way there and back. Remarkably, although six planes were hit, only one aircraft was seen going down. Like themselves on their virgin raid, it was a crew on their very first outing. Plenty of parachutes reassured Mac and co. that they were okay, and they proceeded with confidence to prang the hell out of Gelsenkirchen's Benzol & Coking Plant in retribution.

As February ended and March began, a busy Chedburgh had increased its daylight raid hours to 827 in total, in addition to the 631 night-raid hours that had been completed during the month. The station had contributed over 1,100 tons of bombs, which they had offloaded on the towns and industries of Germany. While there were hopes that the war may be on the home-stretch, the job for Bomber Command was still very much still at full throttle, and March was to be busier still.

Another 1,000 bomber raid on 2 March took Harry's crew to Cologne in *K-King*. Few aircraft were actually able to bomb the target as a result of failures in the transmitter stations, which projected the bombing lines to the aircraft. Their malfunction affected Harry's crew who were among those forced to bring all their bombs home. Described officially as a 'complete failure', the Cologne raid was a bombing disaster. It got worse for Mac's crew, when Harry ordered the crew's 4,000-lb 'cookie' to be dropped in the designated jettison area over the English Channel, entirely unaware that someone else with the same idea was in the process of doing the exact same thing from a position directly above them. Although it scared the life out of them, far from making Mac feel more vulnerable, the continued close shaves with death were only adding to his sense that they were invincible, and that in Harry's hands they would be safe in the skies, always.

Two days later, another 2 a.m. start to Wanne-Eickel called, and stiff opposition awaited. They flew above 10/10ths cloud amid a long stream of barrage for fifteen minutes before reaching the target that was the Marshalling Yard. *L-Love* served Mac and co. well for this day as well as the next, when they returned to Gelsenkirchen to bomb the Schalke Coking Plant. *L-Love*, in spite of a couple of holes being put in her port wing, got the crew there and back in one piece, through the heavy flak. They encountered some German jet fighters *en route*, whose high speeds proved difficult not only for Mac & Ivor, but also for their own pilots. Mac was unable to shoot at them with any real accuracy due to the fact that their movement in and out of range was so fast, but it was also obvious that the fighters' speed rendered them unable to execute any real pursuit tactics themselves. It had been another 3 a.m. start, with little sleep from the previous day, and Mac was exhausted.

On 6 March, they were relieved from ops in order to carry out experiments with a special candle marker, designed to be used when aircraft streams were forming up. Ivor, in the rear turret, operated the candle with switches, and once the candle was lit, it gave the effect of trailing a large coloured flare behind the aircraft. The experiment was a success and the crew moved on to air testing *E-Easy*. That did not go quite so well, as the brake pressure became 'unserviceable' and they were forced into an emergency landing at Woodbridge aerodrome.

The following day, Mac and crew faced their longest trip yet. They were headed to the Russo-German frontier, to Dessau, in an operation that would see them airborne for almost nine and a half hours. It was not a huge success for a number of reasons. A night flight with heavy tail winds resulted in *L-Love* overshooting the target before the markers had been laid down. Ivor, spotting the markers astern from his turret, told Harry to make a turn and they attempted to go around again. By the time they had made the circuit, the attack was over. Their ground speed was negligible as they were flying into fierce headwinds and Harry had to nose down in order to make any progress at all. Eventually reaching their original heading, they released their bombs over the obvious inferno beneath them. There were fighters in the air, so Mac and Ivor were vigilant. *L-Love* was one of the first aircraft to ever be fitted with the new Mk IIc gyro gunsight, and as a result, they were able to spot the silhouette of a Ju 88 against the fires below, to starboard. Ivor set the gunsight and advised Harry to hold their course straight and level, which enabled him to take out the fighter with little problem. Ivor and Mac's kill stats were pretty even, but Ivor was now able to claim the first such loss that anyone had made with the new gunsight.

This small success did not guarantee that the rest of the trip would be without problems, however. It was an exceptionally dark, moonless night, with cloud above and below, and some slightly 'imperfect' navigation put them off course and flying over the one area they had been warned to avoid, Stuttgart. They very nearly paid for this mistake with their lives over what was an intensely hostile region as they found themselves in the middle of the most intense flak they had ever experienced. It came without warning and it was as though every gun in the area had been fired simultaneously. Ivor's rear turret yet again bore the brunt of the attack when flak tore through the Perspex and whipped through his helmet, knocking him out immediately, again. It was terrifying stuff and it was once again due to Harry's expert manipulation of *L-Love* that they got away at all. Returning to base, Mac noticed that his sleeve had a nice hole in it. He was still alive, but it was not just Ivor who had had a near-death experience it seemed, and the damn hole had now ruined his smart Battle Dress.

Another incident free 1,000 bomber raid to Essen followed a few days later, followed by a few days where various members of the crew were dispersed to other duties. On 14 March, Ivor was assigned as mid-upper to another crew for the day. He hated every second of it, feeling entirely unsafe in the hands of another pilot, in a new aircraft. *U-Uncle* was terrible and the pilot was not much better. A thick, industrial fog surrounded them when they returned to base from the raid and, knowing that he and the rest of Harry's crew were due to go on leave the following day, Ivor was determined that they land before any diversions were ordered and he miss his days off. As it happened, Harry was on flying control duty and was doing his best to get them in in a timely fashion. Ivor had to give the pilot of *U-Uncle* his positions, telling him when and where to land, but on their first landing attempt, they almost ended up in a field next to the aerodrome. It took a further two attempts to bring them in successfully, the first of which almost took the whole of flight control with them, but eventually *U-Uncle* was safely brought home. Unfortunately, the incident did nothing but secure *U-Uncle*'s destiny, which was by this time a premature trip to the scrapheap.

While Ivor was having fun realising how lucky Team Warwick were to be crewed together, Mac was on photography runs and air tests. The latter included a ferry flight to the north of France to Juvincourt. A beautiful blue-skied day weather-wise, the trip lifted his spirits in a number of ways. Situated north east of Paris, Juvincourt was a former Luftwaffe airbase that had been captured by the Allies only a few months previously in September 1944. It was now a US Air Force base, which perhaps explained the plentiful presence of tinned pineapples and cream, and oranges as big as footballs. Mac certainly was not complaining as he sat in the sunshine, filling his face with long-missed food, and he set off for his home leave with a lighter mood than he had felt for some time.

He was met by Jean who had managed to venture down from Liverpool to spend a few days with him at home. The kids were thrilled, as always, to see him, and Olive beavered away throughout his short stay cooking, fixing, darning, washing, and ironing his heavy load, so that he could return refreshed.

The two women in his life provided him with such sweet respite during those few days that it was like a medicine for his soul. He was able to set aside temporarily the hideousness of Bill's loss, the strain of the battle, and the constant noise and nerve-

Above left: Olive, Joseph's mother (and my nan), in her favourite chair at the house in Elmdale Grove, with Joe's picture just visible in its place on the china cabinet.

Above right: A very young Olive, before she married and had children.

Right: Joseph (centre) around the age of nine, with younger siblings Dennis and Joyce.

To HARRY MIZLER,
(*Southern Area Lightweight Champion*).

Dear Harry,

Your performance at the National Sporting Club evening when beating the very plucky Al Roth, of A?? been rightly hailed as one of the best of your career.

Your victory has come at the right time. Scep?? beginning to get its hold on many of your admirers must admit, they had grounds for doubting you foll?? rather unimpressive displays against Sarron, Crowle??

You realised that if you could not beat Roth, your?? as a boxer would lose a lot of its former glamour, a?? well understand why there were so many anxious eye?? when you stepped into the ring on Monday.

To our delight, you put up a performance whi?? exaggeration can be ranked in the world champion??

You gave of the best we always knew you posse?? old British boxing stuff, full of brain and clever agg??

You rose to every occasion; you made us feel m??

of you, and you made us feel proud of the gran?? Boxing. Yours was not the ordinary kind of boxi?? a piece of work so beautifully performed that it mi?? cribed in lyrical phrases containing such eulogies "classic"; "rhythm"; "poise" and the last word perfection.

As we watched you shooting out your "straight ?? ing over your "right cross," (and finding your targe?? out of ten) cleverly ducking away from the stormin?? tactics of your rival, and generally displaying the tr?? of the Noble Art, we recalled your brilliant capture o?? weight Championship of Great Britain, at the Alb?? 1934, when you defeated Johnny Cuthbert. There w?? Harry Mizler then—there is only one now.

WE ASK YOU, HARRY, TO KEEP IT UP! Don't suddenly fall back into the pit of letharg?? You know, really, sometimes you do annoy us?? take it into your head to "take it easy" ... you've got

which constitutes the Boxer Perfect and on Monday's ance your chances of winning the championship of ?? are brighter than they have been for a long while.

It's because we KNOW you've GOT IT that we you, for the sake of British Boxing, to KEEP IT UP

Thanks for a grand display, Harry, and thanks fo?? Boxing along.

Above: A cheeky looking Joe, aged around twelve years.

Right: Harry Mizler, champion British boxer
and pleasantly surprising PT coach.

Below left: Mac (left) with close pal and fellow
Joe, 'Smokey' Joe Lee from Liverpool.

Below right: Mac, looking settled and matured in uniform.

Above: Ivor's 14 ITW intake at Bridlington. Joe's intake was number 15 and the two men would later discover that they had a lot more in common, including consecutive service numbers.

Right: Extract from a Browning .303 training manual 1944.

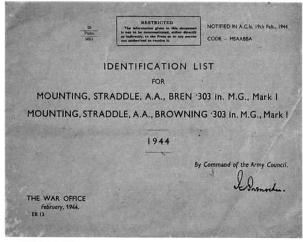

26 Para. 3601	RESTRICTED

RESTRICTED
The information given in this document is not to be communicated, either directly or indirectly, to the Press or to any person not authorised to receive it.

NOTIFIED IN A.C.Is. 19th Feb., 1944

CODE — MSAABBA

IDENTIFICATION LIST

FOR

MOUNTING, STRADDLE, A.A., BREN ·303 in. M.G., Mark I

MOUNTING, STRADDLE, A.A., BROWNING ·303 in. M.G., Mark I

1944

By Command of the Army Council.

THE WAR OFFICE
February, 1944.
EB.13

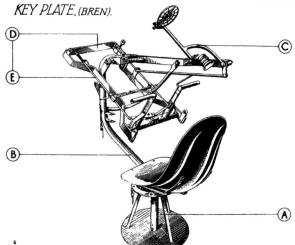

KEY PLATE. (BREN).

Above: The refusal slip received by Olive, declining Joe's request for her dependant's allowance.

Below left: Norman 'Digger' Williams, the inspirational and highly decorated officer under whose tutorship Mac found himself at Bridgnorth.

Below right: Diagram of the hydraulic system of the FN turret which Mac was required to learn.

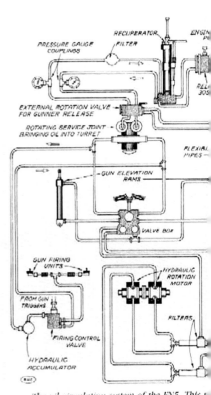

The oil circulation system of the FN5. This is the basic hydraulic circuit of all FN turrets.

Left: Ivor Turley.

Above: Mac's cartoon illustration, clearly expressing the joy he and Joe felt about their coal-hauling experience.

Below: Crewing up: Mac and his newly formed crew-mates.
Back row, left to right: Mac, Bill Perry (bomb aimer), Alec Stott (navigator)
Front row, left to right: Joe Naisbitt (wireless operator), Harry Warwick (pilot), Ivor Turley (rear gunner)

Above left: Harry Warwick and family, post-war.

Above right: A young Brian, my dad.

Below left: A coy-looking Joyce as an older teenager.

Below right: Mac with his beloved Jean at the back of Elmdale Grove.

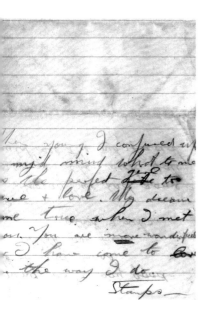

gerry Jones f/K Ken Shaw Nav Joe Lee W/g Alf Robinson M/u H. Thorpes Pat Keyes Pilot Jack Iwin
Lancaster VN - PT 171. 50 sqdn 5 group. Bomber Command. RAF Skellingthorpe.

Above left: The back of one of Olive's letters, which Mac used as scrap paper to rehearse his letter of proposal to Jean.

Above right: Joe Lee and his crew in 50 Squadron.

Below: Extract from the official Flight Operations Record Book, detailing the dramatic events of 12 December 1944, in brief.

Aircraft Type & Number	Crew	Duty	Time Up	Time Down	Details of Sortie or Flight	Reference
LANCASTER I & III.					Bombing - Witten.	A.440.
					Summary - 12 aircraft were detailed and briefed for	Appendix
					operations today. 11 attacked the target, one "Q" failing	
					to return. Cloud was 10/10ths with tops at 15,000 ft.	
					Flak opposition was slight accurate predicted at first,	
					changing to moderate barrage later with scattered bursts	
					from Castrop Rauxel on run in and from Krefeld and Duisburg	
					on way out. 14 fighters (ME 109 & FW. 190's) made beam	
					attacks on main formation but despite this, aircraft	
					maintained a good formation and the bombing appeared	
					concentrated. Aircraft "H" claims 1 ME 109 destroyed.	
					Aircraft "Q" ditched in North Sea 50 miles S.E. of Felixstowe	
					on one engine owing to shortage of petrol. All of the	
					crew were safely rescued without injury.	
G. B.776.	P/O.H.Warwick.	Captain.	11.04.	-----	Bomb load. 1x4000 lb. HC.; 14x500 lb. clusters (4lb) bombs	
	P/O. L. Stott.	Navigator.			Bombed on G.H. aircraft. Aircraft was damaged by heavy flak	
	Sgt. Naismith, J.	Wop/Air.			over target, Nos. 1 and 2 port petrol tanks were badly holed.	
	P/O. W. Ferry.	Air Bomber.			Aircraft was ditched 50 miles off Felixstowe owing to	
	Sgt. Thompson, J.	M.U. Gunner.			shortage of petrol. All the crew were saved.	
	Sgt. Burley, T.	R. Gunner.				
	Sgt. Waring, T.	Flt. Engr.				

Above: The crew, proudly posing with their Lancaster. *From left to right:* Mac, Joe Naisbitt, Alec Stott, Harry Warwick, Tom Waring, Ivor Turley, and 'Windy'.

Below: A view of Northfield, where Olive raised her family as a single parent after the loss of her husband in 1941.

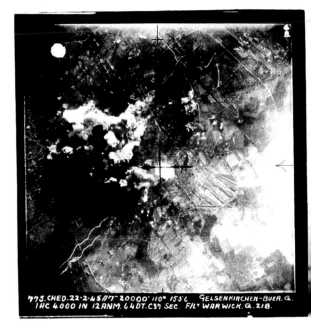

Above left: Newspaper article from the *Cheltenham Chronicle*, 17 February 1945, detailing the tragic loss of Bill Perry.

Above right: Bombing photograph taken from Harry Warwick's crew's aircraft on 22 February 1945 after a bombing raid on Gelsenkirchen.

Below: Operation Manna: a Lancaster is loaded with provisions before a flight to drop supplies over northern Europe.

Above: Birmingham, 1945.

Below: No. 218 Gold Coast Squadron. Mac: third row, dead centre.

Above The only surviving picture of Joseph senior, back row, third from left.

Right: Ivor Turley and bride-to-be Tess.

Below: Britain's heavy snowfall during the winter of 1946–47.

Above left: Mac (right) in his 'nappy', with pals Tex and Jock Brown (front).

Above right: A snap from a rare holiday some time later: Brian, Olive, and Joyce.

Below: Westminster Hospital.

Above left: Olive's handwriting scrawled across the back of the envelope of her eldest son's final letter home, heartbreakingly reads 'last letter'.

Above right: Joseph's final resting place in Northfield, Birmingham.

Below: Olive with my dad, Brian (back left), Dennis, and Joyce, *c.* 1960.

16, Elmdale Grove,
Northfield,
Birmingham, 31.

Mrs. Thompson and family
desire to express their sincere thanks
for your kind sympathy
extended to them
in their sad loss.

September 1947.

Left: The card from Joe's funeral in September 1947, which was returned to me by Harry Warwick's widow.

Below left: Harry Warwick and wife, Joan.

Below right: Ivor Turley and eldest son, Chris.

Right: 'Smokey' Joe Lee on the emotional day when we met in 2014 at an aircrew reunion event.

Below: Myself with dad, Brian, and aunt, Joyce, 2013.

Left: Joyce, 2014.

Below: Olive, my 'Nanny Thompson', holding me in our back garden, late 1967.

jangling of flak. Receiving their nurture, which he craved and they longed to give, was therapeutic indeed, and he hated to have to go.

Leaving Jean and his family and being back in the Chedburgh rut was bad enough, but Mac returned from leave to the discovery that the wing commander had ordered that squadron parades must now take place every morning when there were no battle orders. Unlike at other stations, there would no longer be stand-downs or rest periods for the men who were not on ops, but there was little he could do about it, and moaning would not change a damn thing.

Special training on 23 March was even less fun. There was cloud all the way from 400 to 22,000 feet, bad ice, and an altogether lousy experience. They were Gee-H 'Mouse' bombing, but were forced to abandon after an hour or so due to the weather. The Gee-H equipment had been introduced to Bomber Command the previous spring, and was a means of assisting multiple bomber aircraft in locating and bombing their target with accuracy. Located on the ground in England, a 'Cat' transmitter station would control the track of the aircraft by emitting radio signals to a transponder on the aircraft, and a 'Mouse' station, located elsewhere on UK soil would signal to the aircraft when to release the bombs. Harry's crew had been testing and using this equipment for some time, with varying degrees of success, and training exercises were still a fairly regular occurrence.

Harry and Alec could always be relied upon to keep spirits up, as well as for light relief. Getting roaring drunk was usually where it began. They did not disappoint on the days between ops this week. The pair of them, staggering and shouting, decided it would be entertaining for Mac and his fellow hut-dwellers to be treated to an incursion one evening. Banging their way into the hut, pushing a motorcycle that they had 'borrowed' from who-knows-where, they proceeded to start up the engine and blow on the horn. It was 1 a.m. Their popularity at that particular moment was questionable, but boy did they laugh. The laughter, and the hangovers, lasted throughout the next day.

The longest daylight penetration raid that the RAF had ever attempted was to Hallendorf on 29 March 1945. Harry and crew were one of around 700 aircraft flying in poor weather conditions and thick cloud, which split the formation and doomed the attack. The Met experts made a hash of their predictions and the proposed bombing of the Hermann Göring Steel Works and nearby Benzol installations was unsuccessful. The gunners were all under considerable strain on a six-hour-plus journey through thick cloud, in a formation of so many aircraft, watching for other converging Lancasters. No one really knew where they were, it seemed, and Mac could hear the flak but was not able to see a thing. Many aircraft were seen to be dropping their bombloads in random rural locations, and Harry's crew laughed at the idea that they were all doing their best to put the cows right off their milk that day.

March ended as it had begun, busy and confusing. Chedburgh's numbers had increased, with 1,367 tons of bombs being dropped and 1,680 hours of operational flying hours in the bag.

C H E D

10.30 pm Thursday

Hello "Boofull" Well first
of all we got back O.K.
Mom as you can see.
We were were on that
big of last night to
Chemnitz but we had to
come back before we'd ever
crossed the battle line
in the south of France.
One of our engines cut-out
but we got back on 3 O.K.
Alec our navigator is
in hospital with sinus
trouble. I pity him 'cos I've
had it and its hellish
painfull.
He fainted from it once

on our way back from
Dortmund.

By the way Mom, will
you try and find out
what shows there are on
at the "Hipp" & Royal I
think it is. In time for my
leave as I would like
Jean to come down to our
place this next leave, is
it OK with you?

I will send you the money
for the tickets so that
you can book them for me
if you will.

Whilst on the subject of
money I'm enclosing a £1
for you to help you out
with whatever needs
it most. Its not for the

theatre tickets but for
you.
If I don't write much
this time I hope you
will excuse me as I'm
feeling pretty low. I don't
know what's the matter
with me today.
Jean has been going this
hell with her feet, I
don't know what she's
done. Has that knee of yours
got any better?
Well good-night & God-
bless. Keep smiling, I do.

Love *[signature]* sorry about
the pencil
x x x

12

Joyce is Hospitalised

Olive
Northfield, Birmingham
April 1945

While Joe had been on constant Battle Orders, Olive was struggling to make ends meet, working as many hours as she could, and feeling stressed and irritable. When she received an official looking letter marked 'on his majesty's service' that contained another disappointing confirmation that her Dependant's Allowance request had been declined, she felt worse. As often as he could, Joe popped £1 into an envelope and told his mum to use it as she saw fit. Their financial situation was very difficult—that was undeniable—but Olive was learning to become a master of thrift, and it was increasingly requiring all her wits and effort to manage the household on the meagre budget that she could afford.

Although she was now used to struggling, especially since she had been widowed, the situation was particularly tight when there were three hungry, growing children in the house and the curse of rations to contend with. It had been a long winter and the kids had been impeccably behaved during the weeks of indoor confinement. Save for their disastrous annual trip to the Panto, where they had queued for two hours for tickets, only to find someone else sitting in their seats, the only relief for the kids had come in the form of heavy snowfall. January had been freezing and the snow had provided Joyce and Brian with a perfect playground. They had sledged until their hands and feet had been so cold that they were forced back indoors to defrost. Once fed and warmed up again, there would be little that could stop them from donning their balaclavas, still damp from their steamy breath around the mouth hole, and heading back out to build snow barricades and rejoin the snowball fights. With hard effort, the little blighters had turned the slope of the Grove into an ice-slide, which had provided them with enormous fun and many bruises for several days, even if it had created a treacherous obstacle course for the older residents of the neighbourhood who had been forced to keep their wits about them for the many snow-induced hazards that littered their path, until the thaw came.

The weather was now much warmer and spring was here. Olive was glad of it. She had been missing Joe badly and had been pleased to see him on his most recent leave, even if these days she had to share his time with Jean too. She did still worry about the girl, in spite of her growing fondness for her. She was very young but not very tough when Olive compared her with her own self at the same age. She was aware that Jean had been off sick from her job recently for almost three weeks, as a result of what the doctor had apparently described as 'nervous debility'. Granted, there was a war on and it had consumed a full five-plus years of Jean's young life, but this was still a generation who had it a whole lot easier than Olive had as a youngster, with so many siblings and so little money. It was difficult to imagine what a teenager like Jean could possibly have to be depressed about. No doubt she too was missing Joe during his long absences and worrying for his safety, but it would help her enormously if Joseph could try to entice her into taking up some kind of a skill or hobby. It would be therapeutic and help her to pass the time in a productive way. Better, however, that the advice did not come directly from her to Jean, she decided, but that Joe be the intermediary to offer counsel to his fiancée.

The kids were playing marbles as she tried to write to her eldest son with her idea. Joyce and Brian were arguing and cheating, making plenty of noise and she knew it must be time for bed. They had had a disturbed night the previous evening as, for the first time in months, the air raid sirens had gone off. She was unconvinced by the urgency and did not get out of bed while they continued to sound for a further twenty minutes or so. The children had not roused either, although Olive still kept a small mattress in the lobby beneath the stairs for the children to sleep on, should the need arise.

Unable to sleep now, Olive's thoughts turned to her thirteen-year-old daughter who had been suffering with a painful injury to her knee for the past few weeks. A month or so previously, Joyce had slipped during a gymnastics lesson at school while trying to leap over the 'horse'. It had deteriorated so badly that she was now facing the prospect of surgery in order to correct it. The doctor had initially thought it to be a knee injury and had suspected that there might be a torn ligament, but after several weeks there was little improvement, so Olive had asked for an X-ray to be taken. This had necessitated a trip into Birmingham city centre to the Orthopaedic Hospital, where it transpired that it was actually Joyce's hip rather than her knee that was the problem, and was causing the symptoms in her leg. A 'slipped epiphysis' to the right hip was diagnosed; it would require 'realignment'. Olive had been horrified to hear what her daughter's treatment would consist of, and had decided to keep the details from Joyce, for fear of terrifying her. It was not clear whether her hip would even respond to the proposed course of action, but what choice did they have but to go through with it, or run the risk of seeing Joyce become crippled as she grew older?

The operation she would undergo would attempt to correct her hip placement, and she would then be encased in plaster from her waist to her toes for a significant period of time. She would then essentially be weighted down and periodically turned and 'stretched' on a rotating bed, with her feet raised, in the hope that it would eventually correct her alignment and gait. It all sounded primitive and painful to Olive, who was sick with concern that another of her children would be leaving the family home for a while and she wondered how she would manage without her.

Her daily life was getting more and more busy, and the loss of Joyce, who was such a diligent and sensible girl, would be another major hole in family life. There were countless jobs to do around the house. The fowl were now laying well, in fact producing ten eggs from ten hens per day, far too many to eat, so Olive needed to once again set about preserving them for the winter before they went bad. These were the tasks that Joyce usually helped her with, but she would just have to manage alone this time.

Joyce entered hospital on 14 April 1945. Although Joyce did not know it, it was expected that her hospitalisation would last a minimum of six months. Only two nibs now. She would miss every hair of her head.

To add to this depressing thought, Olive had heard nothing from Joe for almost two weeks since she had written to her son with her characteristic forthright and unsympathetic advice about Jean's depression. She was finding it hard to subdue the anger that she was feeling with him, being certain that his absence of correspondence was a petulant way of punishing her for her words by ignoring her letter. Surely he knew how anxious she would be in the absence of his regular mail? On top of the situation with money and now Joyce, it was really too much.

While she knew that Joe's most recent letters had held a melancholy tone, and that he was well into his ops now, she was still frustrated. Olive was trying hard to shake off the feeling of being sorry for herself, but wondered how her life had become such a chore. Her husband was gone, the country was at war, food was scarce, her firstborn son was in mortal danger, and now her only daughter was being taken from her too. She wondered how little Brian would miss his sister's presence, they were such close playmates the two of them.

In reality, Joe was riddled with fatigue and he had been so busy working and trying to grab sleep when and where he could that he had had no time to write or to harbour any feelings of ill will towards his mother. The appalling speed with which mail was arriving at Chedburgh had also played a part, since it was impossible to answer letters that he had not even received. In addition to fighter affiliation duties, with which he had been so out of practice that he had felt a little air sick, there had also been bombing exercises between ops.

Following their long daylight raid on Hallendorf, there had been no op for Joe and crew until 4 April, when they had been sent on a night raid to Leuna, near Leipzig. The target had been some synthetic oil plants, successfully bombed through fairly heavy cloud. Their twentieth operation had gained them another plaudit, and news reached them that, as a result of their continued success as a crew, receiving 'good' recommendations on sixteen out of twenty of their raids, they had earned themselves a reduction in their tour total. They would now only be required to complete thirty operations. Although the war seemed only to be heading in one direction now, there was still plenty of fighting expected to be done across Germany, so Joe was optimistic that they would be able to complete their tour without going overseas.

On Friday night, 13 April, 218 Squadron conducted a raid on Kiel, situated in the north of Germany, close to the border with Denmark and edging the Baltic Sea. The stream bombed and sunk the German cruiser *Admiral Scheer*, causing much celebration among the ranks of 218 Squadron.

The following night they headed back into the Berlin ring of defences, attacking a target a little east of Potsdam. Innumerable searchlights and very heavy flak greeted them, and once leaving the flak area, there were fighters in waiting, making for another nerve-shattering eight-plus hours in the black skies over Europe.

Consolation came in the form of a promotion. Joe was now a flight sergeant and he felt he had very much deserved it.

The weather turned hot and sunny. Munich served up clear skies and a discreet, small number of Lancaster crews were selected for the target, including Harry's. The excellent visibility gave Joe a bird's eye view of the American 7th Army converging upon Nuremberg. It was quite a sight, but not as magnificent as his view of the Alps and Lake Constance, which he found spellbinding.

Olive spent many hours thinking about him and his worries. The hot, blue skies of mid-April rewarded her with a thrill as she heard the unmistakable hum of a Lancaster overhead one morning. She gazed upwards, calling Brian and Dennis to wave, and they wondered out loud whether it could be Joe up there, thrilled by the thought that he might be so close.

After all this time, she still found it incredibly helpful to hear from him, to see his writing and understand his woes. It eased her thoughts to be able to be a mother for him, however distant; to be able to contemplate where he was and what he was doing and to have him share his troubles in a letter. He told her repeatedly not to worry. Any mother reading his letters would understand the absurdity of such a platitude; what else can a mother do but worry?

Joyce's confinement was also dominating her mind and her time. She was in the Royal Orthopaedic Hospital, locally known as The Woodlands. Being in Northfield and thankfully a straightforward tram ride away from home, Olive was hoping to visit daily and was devastated to be told that visiting hours were on Sundays only, for one and a half hours. She made a pact with Joyce that she would try to sneak in more often. She did not disappoint.

On the first visiting day, Olive had found her daughter in good spirits, but she was distressed to see how her daughter was positioned in her bed. Her torso was encased in a plaster cast from waist to toe and was tied to the top and bottom of her bed, upon which a wide board had been placed. Tilted at a severe angle, her head below her feet, she lay in the bed in a reversed position, with her feet at the head end. Olive wished for all she was worth that she could take her daughter's place, but tried to console herself with the knowledge that this was the only course of action that might prevent Joyce from ending up with a permanent disability.

On some days, she would make extra egg sandwiches and cram them in to her lunch box before setting off to her work at the Austin. When lunchtime came, she would catch the bus or tram to the hospital and smuggle the eggy treats into the ward to distribute among Joyce and the other girls with whom she was imprisoned.

When Joe heard the news about Joyce, he was shocked. Olive had initially considered not worrying him with the news, but once it had become clear that it would be a long-term recovery process, she had had to come clean. He felt sick to think of the situation in which his long-suffering little sister now found herself, with such restricted movement and without frequent family visitation or school friends nearby.

The nurses assured Olive that she would receive schooling and get plenty of fresh air, so she would be well occupied during her stay. Olive had bought her a dressing gown with the £1 that Joe had sent and it fitted a treat. She was overwhelmed by Joyce's sunny attitude and tolerance of her situation. She really was a little brick, never complaining, despite her discomfort. Unable to sleep in such a difficult position, however, the nurses had now provided Joyce with sleeping powders, enough to give a little relief for a short while.

Entertainment in the ward came in the form of an elderly gentleman pianist, who arrived each Saturday evening and proceeded to play tunes while everyone talked over him. The school work was almost pointless—the girls in the ward ranged in age so wildly that it was impossible for the lessons to be relevant to anyone. At least they had fishcakes to look forward to at breakfast time—yuk.

Dennis was busy saving his wages for the annual YMCA holiday in the Lake District. Brian was missing Joyce so much that he had taken to following Olive about the house like a shadow, and they sat down daily together to compose a letter to her. Jean was also writing to Joyce and Olive pleaded with Joe that they both keep a positive and sunny tone in their correspondence.

The 22nd marked the anniversary of the death of Joseph senior, Olive's husband. It had been four years since he had passed suddenly in bed beside her. It was on all of their minds. April was surely their 'black' month and this year it was living up to its reputation in spades. On a visit to see Joyce, Olive was accompanied by her sisters, Lill and Phyl, along with Phyl's long-awaited and beloved baby daughter, Judith. In a horrifying turn of events, six-week-old Judith was suddenly taken desperately ill, fitting and turning a deathly colour. It was a complete mystery, and Phyllis, in a state of near collapse with panic, could only offer the observation that the little girl had been a bit quieter than normal that morning. A doctor came immediately, so disturbed by the apparent proximity to death of baby Judith that he put her into his own car and drove her to Selly Oak Hospital's emergency department himself, for fear that a decision to wait for an ambulance might prove a fatal one. Olive had never seen a child so close to death before, and she had waited, stealing herself for the worst news to follow. She thanked God that the doctor had acted so quickly, and that Judith's condition had been stabilised in hospital. In time she would make a full recovery, but this was a month that Olive never wished to repeat.

May must surely be an improvement upon the month just passed. The end of this terrible war was finally in sight and Olive had faith in the news reels which were indicating that the Jerries would be giving up soon. She hoped so, for the sake of her family. They could not bear another loss.

Joyce was thirteen years old when she entered hospital. The war that had acted as a permanent backdrop to her childhood was still raging. She could not have known that she would be fourteen before she learned to walk again, or that the next time she saw her own home the war would be long over.

16 Elmdale Grove
Northfield
Sunday night

Dear Joseph,

I can't start my letter by thanking you for yours this time as I have not heard from you for nearly a fortnight, but I do hope all is well with you. I know you are kept fully occupied but it would be a relief to have if only a short letter to set my mind at rest. I suppose I hurt your feelings when I wrote about Jean as I did, but in your heart of hearts & knowing you as I do, I think you will agree with what I said. In any case I have got more than enough worry on my mind at the moment without you deliberately adding to it, as I am expecting to have to take Joyce in the Woodlands hospital some time this week to have an operation on her hip. I took her to the doctors a month ago & he said it was the ligament in her knee that it was damaged & as there was no improvement — in fact it was getting worse — I asked if I could have an X ray or some further advice, so he gave me a note to take her to Broad St. where I was told that her hip was damaged but not diseased. It may respond to treatment but they don't think so, in any case you are not to worry as she will be in good hands & I will write you as soon as I know anything else. She is quite bright & is not at all worried by the prospect, but of course she doesn't know all the details. The rest of us are alright & I do hope you are. Aunties Lill, Emma & Phyll. came this afternoon & they all asked about you. As I came back from seeing them on the tram, Leo Terry came home & nobody expecting him. He looked fitter & fatter than I have ever seen him. The hens continue to deliver the goods & I have started to preserve some ready for the winter. I nearly forgot but I received the enclosed some time last week, so it looks as if we might as well leave things as they are. Well I'll close now son & say good night & God bless you always.

Love from Mother & nibs. x x x x x x

13

The Beginning of the End

Mac
RAF Chedburgh
1 May–31 May 1945

The raids on Kiel harbour were among the last for the whole of Bomber Command. Motivated by fears that the Germans were preparing ships to transport soldiers to Norway to continue the fighting that was so clearly coming to an end across Europe, the port of Kiel and the ships coming and going from that area became the final targets for bombing campaigns as April drew to a close.

Mac and the boys took some scheduled leave toward the end of the month. Mac took a train to Liverpool, which he caught by the skin of his teeth, in thanks only to its tardiness. He arrived at Lime Street, in spite of his failure to communicate the train times to Jean, to find her waiting at the station with her little sister, Mary. Female intuition, no doubt. As they did the rounds of visiting relatives, whose repeated enquiries about Joyce's health Mac found extremely touching, a German radio announcement stopped them and the rest of the nation in its tracks. Adolf Hitler, it said, was dead.

While Mac and the rest of the British public had no details as to either the validity or the circumstances of Hitler's demise, it seemed promising. Churchill did not comment.

In actual fact, with growing panic at the encroaching Russian and American ground forces, as well as his apparent betrayal by Himmler, Hitler believed that Berlin was in danger of falling imminently, and that the end was inevitable for his 1,000-year Reich. On 29 April, Hitler had learned of the death by execution of his ally Mussolini. Reports reached him that the bodies of Mussolini and his mistress had been publicly mutilated, a fate which had horrified the Führer. Appointing Admiral Dönitz as his successor, with orders to continue Germany's fight against the Bolsheviks, Hitler had married his girlfriend, Eva Braun, in a private ceremony in the Berlin bunker which they had occupied for some months. Their suicides had followed within hours—his by gunshot wound to the head, hers by cyanide pill.

As instructed, their bodies had been led outside and, using petrol, set alight. The bunker was captured just two days later and it was said that it would be only a matter of days before the end would be official.

Mac returned to Chedburgh on 3 May and was greeted by a number of Olive's baking triumphs, now bone-hard but still enticing enough to be considered edible, and as such, consumed, with a little help from the boys, without ceremony. No. 218 Squadron felt different. There were no battle orders, but assignments to a new kind of operational duty now filled their logbooks.

On 7 May, Mac and the crew heard of the full and unconditional surrender of the German forces to the Allies. The end had seemed to come quickly. Since mid-April, as British and US ground troops had advanced, news broadcasts had announced a succession of liberations, including the concentration camps at Bergen-Belsen and Dachau. The horrifying nature of the suffering of so many thousands of innocent people at the hands of the Nazis had subsequently begun to become clear. Even liberation was unable to save some of them, who were so far along the route to starvation or infection with disease that they could not be saved.

The attention of Bomber Command was now turning to relief operations. Mac, Harry, and crew experienced their first sortie under Operation Manna a day later on 8 May. Targeted at the still-occupied western area of the Netherlands, where vast numbers of the population were feared to be nearing starvation, Manna was a coordinated attempt to ensure that humanitarian food drops, uncontested by German opposition, be allowed to take place in the famine-hit areas. Supported by Operation Chowhound, a similar humanitarian mission by the US Air Force, bomber squadrons were now being mobilised to transport the food cargo packages to Holland. An agreed ceasefire commenced on 30 April 1945. As these sorties would be uncontested, air crews were unable to record the flying hours toward their operational targets in their logbooks, which for Mac meant that he would inevitably be unable to complete his intended 'tour'.

The food drops, known affectionately as 'Spam Raids', required extremely low flying at around 500 feet, since the cargo packages were without parachutes. Parcels consisted of tinned goods, dried food, and chocolate bars and the bomb bays of the Lancaster bombers were stuffed full with their new benign loads before their onward transfer to the famine-riddled areas of Holland.

Now manned with a crew of just five men, a bomb aimer and rear gunner being redundant on such uncontested runs, Mac's first Spam Raid took him to The Hague. They were one of eight Chedburgh crews sent to drop thirty-six enormous food aid packages. The packages were dropped in two main locations: at the airfield near Ypenburg and at the Duindigt racecourse, both providing wide open spaces large enough to safely drop the cargo, which was an inexact science. Crowds were, however, invariably waiting, and at such low altitudes, it was possible for the bomber crews to see clearly how their food parcels were received. Flags and signs had been prepared by the waiting Dutch citizens, who cheered and waved madly as the aircraft flew by. It was quite a sight for Mac, who was struck by the sudden and complete change in the nature of his duties, from hostile and deadly, to positive and emotionally rewarding, overnight.

The food was intended for distribution among the local population, but there was often the temptation for the starving recipients to break into the parcels immediately. This did not always end well, as other crews witnessed, as the sudden binge eating sometimes caused vomiting in those who were too eager to get started. By the time Manna and Chowhound were completed, supported on the ground by Operation Faust, during which Allied trucks also transported humanitarian aid, over 3,000 sorties would have been made, delivering a total of 11,000 tons of food.

Mac's first Spam Raid had taken place on VE Day. He was desperate to hear how the rest of British civilisation had been celebrating the event, but was mindful of the fact that Joyce was still imprisoned in her hospital ward, like himself with little hope of joining in the festivities in the streets at home.

In actual fact, the residents of Elmdale Grove had excelled themselves. Olive was enjoying a rare two-day holiday from work and the excitement was palpable. Her mood was high, in spite of her regrets that her family was not together for such a momentous occasion, and she carried a warmth and enormous pride with her when she read of her eldest son's newest operational duties. To know that the aircraft that had been created and utilised for mass destruction were now occupied on such worthwhile humanitarian errands filled her with joy. She had prayed for the end and it had finally come. It was a relief that she found hard to articulate, but the knowledge that her boy had survived the battles and trauma of it all was as if a pressure had been lifted from her after the longest time.

The houses in and around Olive's street had all been decorated with paper bunting and the residents' *pièce de résistance* came in the form of a life-sized Guy-Fawkes-style dummy of Adolf Hitler, which had been hung on the lamp post at the bottom of the Grove. Beneath its feet a large pile of wood and kindling had been laid, in readiness for the fake Führer as darkness fell. His fate would be fiery and merciless, in Northfield at least. She had heard that the town centre was beautifully decorated and was to be floodlit that evening, so perhaps she would escape the festivities here and take Brian to see the real deal later on.

As for Joyce, she had celebrated VE Day without her family, although the nurses had taken the time to decorate the ward to cheer things up a bit for the girls who were held captive within. Her highlight had been a trip to the window where she had been able to catch a glimpse of the Victory Tram making its way, illuminated, along the Bristol Road. She was feeling a great deal brighter, maximising the visits from her mum and brothers every Sunday, and looking forward to the promised X-ray, which the ward sister had hoped would show signs of improvement in her hip. VE Day had brought treats for the girls in the ward—two fishcakes for breakfast instead of the usual one, and tinned plums for pudding. A small orchestra had provided the soundtrack for a mammoth 'singathon' and they had all been hoarse by the time the lights had been turned out.

Joyce was not escaping from school lessons while in the Woodlands. Miss Marjerrison was efficient and kind as a teacher, but was challenged by the conditions and the diversity of her pupils. Not only were some, like Joyce, tied to a bed at an inverted angle, but their ages were widespread. When the weather was kind she arranged for the girls who were in awkward positions to be released for a short while, and she took their lessons outside. The fresh air was welcome, but Joyce knew instinctively that it was all a waste of time. Her only positive news was the promise that the weights at the end of her legs would be removed by the end of the month.

While the world was celebrating Victory in Europe, Mac's work continued. Once the Spam Raids were over, duties had now turned to the increasing number of newly-liberated POW camps, from which former prisoners were spilling in vast numbers. Operation Exodus was a coordinated effort to repatriate the growing numbers of ex-POWs to the UK. Bomber Command aircraft, freed from their bombing raid duties, were now employed in the transit of people, and Mac's crew set out on their first of these sorties on 10 May.

Their destination was Juvincourt in Northern France, a familiar airbase for Mac, who had spent a pleasant afternoon eating pineapple in the sun there some weeks back. The assumption that this would be an 'easy trip' was accurate in some ways, but fell short of the mark in others. Operation Exodus was to provide the bomber crews with an exhausting and incessant series of double sorties, ferrying men from France and Belgium back to the receiving centres across the UK. Sleep would be hard to come by for the foreseeable future, and the emotional impact of their close interactions with these newly-released prisoners would be unexpectedly difficult.

On a daily basis from their first sortie on 10 May, Mac's crew flew to Juvincourt or Belgium to collect POWs, returned them to the UK, usually to RAF Westcott in Buckinghamshire, returned to base, and then repeated the trip once more. They did not find their beds until 10.30 p.m., but were woken at 1.30 a.m. to do the whole thing again. Such was the frenetic nature of this period that Mac wrote to Olive in a short tea break from RAF Westcott on the back of a Nav map, the only paper he could lay his hands on, courtesy of Alec.

No. 218 Squadron were repatriating 200–500 ex-POWs every day, at the slow rate of twenty-four per aircraft, per trip. Mac and crew were provided with strict instructions to seat their sorry passengers in specific places on the Lancaster, and the numbers were strictly limited to twenty-four. An early, fatal accident during Exodus had illustrated the dangers of allowing the weight of twenty-four extra passengers to sit in the rear of the aircraft. A Lancaster had taken off from Juvincourt, but its passengers had disrupted the aircraft's flight trim, causing the pilot to lose control. They had crashed and all passengers and crew had perished as a result.

Mac and crew carried twenty-four Mae Wests and a similar number of blankets on each trip. Their passengers were marshalled on board and spread out along the full length of the fuselage, then strictly reminded to stay seated. The faces of the men who boarded their aircraft were often emaciated, sometimes joyous, but often so wracked with the emotion of going home after so long in captivity that they were unable to hide their relief. Many burst into tears before they entered the Lancaster, others cried as they crossed the English coastline, all were invariably in terrible shape physically.

There were always hundreds of men awaiting the roll-call of passengers at the airfields from which the crews collected their human cargo. Not all of them would make it onto the twenty-four-limit flights on the same day, and although they waited in patient groups, their palpable excitement and high expectations were obvious. Mac's conversations with these long-suffering men were illuminating. Many of them had been on forced marches of 700 or 800 miles in bitter winter conditions across Poland and Germany, moved by German troops who were fleeing the advancing Russian Army. They had watched their already-weak and starving colleagues die on the roadside from the lack of rations, cold, pneumonia, or disease. Some spoke of England as a place that Mac hardly recognised, such was their now-fantastical memory of home after prolonged absence. Their clothing was in tatters and they were filthy. He watched as some fell to the floor upon exiting their kite, clasping their hands and kissing the ground. Medics greeted the arriving aircraft, squirting the occupants, POWs, and crew alike with their anti-mosquito Flit guns front and back, then leading them to the waiting hangars.

It was emotional. The long tables of food and beverages that greeted their passengers were strictly for POWs only. God knows they needed it. Mac felt an intense and growing sense of gratification with each of these journeys. These men had suffered and he had helped them get home. Those POWs well enough to travel would be fed, passed on to a transit camp nearby where they could be supplied with new battle dress, take a bath, get a shave, and find a bed to sleep in before being provided with a railway warrant, some cigarettes, and £5 cash in order to make their onward respective journeys home to their families.

By the time Operation Exodus was finished, 72,500 POWs would be repatriated, across 2,900 separate missions. The devastation of the European airfields, ironically the excellent work of Bomber Command in most cases, had to be undone before many of the Exodus sorties could take place. Exodus lasted approximately one month.

Mac's crew took part in one of the final sorties of Exodus on 27 May. They had company in the shape of Group Captain Brotherhood, who joined them as a redundant bomb aimer for the ride. Best behaviour required. The weather was hot in May and Mac found himself thinking that it was Blighty's way of greeting her lost boys, offering them a perfect specimen of British weather to come home to.

Once the prisoners had all been brought home, the flying continued with other unusual passengers on board. Pleasure trips for the ground crew at Chedburgh were now taking place. As with everything in the RAF, the boys were nicknaming these excursions as 'Cook's Tours', the RAF bomber crews providing the Thomas Cook-like travel agency experiences, which would enable the non-flying personnel to see the efforts to which they had also so diligently contributed. Harry took off on their first Cook's Tour with a long itinerary planned. A seven-hour flight would introduce their passengers to Aachen, Koblenz, Cologne, Düren, Bonn, Frankfurt, Kassel, Hanover, Hamburg, Bremen, Osnabrück, Dortmund, Essen, Witten, Duisburg, Düsseldorf, and Wesel. The nostalgia began to bite as they flew over Witten, with recollections of that first disastrous mission six months ago, and the ground crew personnel on board were able to witness first-hand how much damage had been inflicted by these enormous, faithful aircraft that they had kept aloft for the duration of the war in Europe.

By the time May had ended, the crew had lost another member. Joe Naisbitt, the wireless operator, had been posted on to Transport Command. As yet, Mac had no idea exactly where he was headed other than a base somewhere in Yorkshire. Their new W/O was an Australian who seemed like a decent bloke, but boy did he miss Joe.

While the end of hostilities was a huge relief and the crew were relishing their new peace-time humanitarian duties, it seemed to Mac that peacetime was sending the RAF back into the familiar territory of red-tape and discipline. His permanent promotion to flight sergeant became official on 29 May, and he was faced with the prospect of considering what he wanted to do with his life after the war. There were vocational training opportunities now on offer and Mac was thinking about signing up for some, not because he was actively motivated to take up a new trade, but because it seemed churlish not to accept something that was on offer, for free. A passive approach to wood machinery training probably was not the model of positivity, he knew, but he might as well put his name down for something.

As it turned out, he was soon distracted by a different opportunity, as a chance arose for him to train as a gunnery instructor. Casting his mind back to the battle-hardened veterans who had provided him with so much information and inspiration when he was learning the ropes himself, he knew immediately that he would sign up. Ivor and one other flight sergeant joined him on the course, and Mac loved it. It would take a few weeks to qualify, and exams would follow, but he would then be able to teach new RAF recruits the art of gunnery, which he had mastered both at peace and in combat.

CMEO again.
Sunday

Dear Mom,

Well after what seems like weeks I can sit down & write a letter. Hope you did not worry too much over the absence of letters from me; but as they say "no news is good news".

We've been doing two trips a day to the Continent to fetch back our Ex.P.O.W.s & it's not even given me time for a regular wash! Our meals we ate when we could (get 'em!) & sleep was indeed a luxury!

Still, we felt it was all worth while when we saw the looks of the chaps faces as they set foot on England after so long. Some cried others laughed & whooped like kids & others just looked & looked drinking in the surrounding country of the various dromes they were set down at. I was glad the weather was nice for their home coming & it was of a sort they all dreamed of for years as they were rotting in the camps & stalags. Most of them are in a bad shape & their spirit completely

gone. I felt as we all
do very sorry for them
yet glad of the fact
they can be with
there folks. I looked
out for Norman Mallen as
you can guess but did
not see him. He's
probably changed as you'd
say. Nearly all of 'em have
been of on 600 + 800 mile
forced marches.
That's enough of that
for now. I'd got your
letter when I got back
+ was glad to see that
Joyce is feeling a little
better + is getting
more sleep. I must write
to her. Hows Judith now?

I hardly dare write to
"57" & ask as its so
long since last I wrote
yet I'm always promising.
(Aunt Em too)
Your end its many
writing to one, and with
me its one writing to
many. I hope they under-
stand.

Well this is about all
for now so God – bless
& Keep Smiling, I do.
Don't worry over me, I'm fine

Toodle – oo.

P.S. Hope to
come on
leave on the
13th June.
That's up to now
anyway !!

14

Relationship Troubles

Olive
Northfield, Birmingham
1 June 1945–31 July 1945

True to form, June brought rain and lots of it. Olive had a stinker of a cold and discovered that Joe, Jean, and most other people she knew shared in her gloom. She quipped with the children, in family tradition, that they would be declared better only once they could say 'string'.

She wondered whether the sudden illness was her body's way of giving in to the relief that had engulfed her following the end to the hostilities. It was impossible to adequately express her current feelings about Joe. Appeasement that his active operations were over, at least for the time being, but much more than that. As she had read his account of the recent sorties under Operation Exodus, she had brimmed with pride. The satisfaction she felt knowing that her son was bringing home those who had been imprisoned away from home for so long was enormous. The men had suffered terribly and she hoped that Joe would be touched with a similar sense of gratification to her own for carrying out this honourable task.

Relief had also come for her anxieties over Joyce. In the first week of June, the top part of her plaster cast had been removed, due in part to the presence of some nasty sores on her skin. Although she was still tied down, she had now been without the plaster cast for a whole week and Olive knew it must feel like heaven to feel the air on her skin. She looked very thin, although sleep was proving easier to find as she had finally been allowed a pillow. Now moved to a new, flat bed, she had also at last been released from the inverted angle that had been so terribly uncomfortable and allowed to lay in a normal position. The new bed was not without its own torture equipment, however. Designed to pull much harder on the long-suffering Joyce's legs, it did exactly that. Olive was amazed by her daughter's capacity to tolerate the unbearable, and never failed to smile at her ever-pleasant mood when she visited. She was full of impish mischief with the nurses and was always conspiring with her fellow patients to torment them in one way or another. Their latest favourite scheme was to pretend to be vomiting and call with a sense of urgency for a nurse. Seeing the hapless Nurse Ream falling for their tricks time and again, running breathlessly around the ward to attend to the sick patient, gave the naughty girls a great deal of shameless pleasure. It was amazing, thought Olive, what games bored children could cook up, given enough free time. Olive promised Joyce a holiday by the seaside the moment she was released from her jail.

Joe was due on leave on 13 June and he had promised to come home, asking permission for Jean to join him once more. While she was happy for Jean to visit, she was frustrated by the deplorable ration situation and irritated by the youngsters' lack of acknowledgment of how far she stretched things to cater for the family. With Joyce in hospital, there may be one less mouth to feed, but she wondered whether she had perhaps done too good a job of protecting the nibs, including Joe, from the reality of just how hard she had to work to make it appear as though they had plenty. Joe's leave periods were always preceded by weeks of saving, baking, preserving and scrimping in order to treat him in the manner to which he had become accustomed on leave. Her intention was always to fill his heart with motherly love and his belly with motherly fare. She only hoped that Jean would have the sense to bring her ration card with her, but decided not to leave this to chance. She began a letter to Joe, making sure he had it firmly front of mind. Current allowances provided her with only 9 ounces of bacon per week and 3 ounces of fat, to share between them. In previous months, Freda, who had worked at the local shop, had always popped in a bit of 'extra' for Olive, feeling sorry for the widow raising four kids alone in wartime. Freda no longer worked at the shop, however, so rations were rations.

Signing off on her latest note, she made a quick mental calculation of the number of days until his leave. The simple action of counting down transported her immediately back to his childhood, when they would count the sleeps until Christmas. Smiling and without consciously thinking about it, she wrote out the initials of the seven remaining days until he would be home, and planted a 'kiss' beneath each. She wondered whether he would understand this private language, and although she knew it was childish, it made her feel good.

Joe's leave came and went without incident. His mother had chastised both Joe and Jean for keeping late hours, but the days simply had not been long enough to waste time with sleep. He had wanted to wring every possible moment out of the week with Jean and the late evenings had provided them with some precious alone time. He was back on base with his fiancée's sweet scent still in his nostrils by 20 June.

The inactivity at Chedburgh following the Exodus missions was getting Joe and the rest of the crew down. The hut was a hive of inertia and the men were pottering on unnecessary or unwelcome tasks that they had been putting off for months. Tom, having declared himself a champion darner, was crucifying another pair of some poor unsuspecting chap's socks. He had turned his well-meaning attentions earlier in the day to Mac's, but when Mac had come to try them on his heel, he had been surprised to find a large lump constructed from what appeared to be a full half pound of the wrong-coloured wool. He was now walking with a pronounced limp, but it had been worth it just for the hysteria that had ensued. Tom was still at it, but Joe made a mental note to ask Olive next time.

The few flights that they had had since Exodus were all benign, moving aircraft around, air to air firing practice, fighter affiliation, and so forth. Less than five hours in the air in June so far. Now that they were back they got a few more hours in on mock raids and H2S Radar test flights, and the training seemed to be cranking up a notch, but he was strangely missing the conflict. This H2S flight would be the last hours that Joe would record in his logbook, although he was a long way from knowing so at that moment.

The long faces at Chedburgh were matched and exceeded in Northfield when Olive received the shaking news that Joe may soon be posted to Burma. While the news reports were optimistic about the war with Japan, Burma was still a hot-bed of fighting, and Olive was concerned. Joe clearly felt more ambivalent about the situation, fearing not for himself, but for the two women who had been waiting patiently for his return, only to discover that he may now be sent overseas for a long stretch. Olive's advice was to keep this news from Jean, fearing that it would bring her down. Joe rejected this idea out of hand. Her instincts were of course protective, but Joe was confident that it was always better to have the full facts, no matter how hard to hear. How, he reminded her, would he have felt if he had come home to unexpectedly discover that his little sister was in hospital, strapped to a bed, with the prospect of staying there, as a prisoner, for months to come? Olive conceded.

A few days later, at the end of June, Joe was able to temporarily put her mind at rest about the potential imminence of any overseas tour, although he managed to blow her mind with other news.

Burma, it seemed, would be at least a few months away, since it had now been announced that all air crews with twenty or more completed battle operations would be grounded mandatorily for a period of five months from the date of their last operation. Their last op to Bremen had been on 22 April, meaning that Olive and Jean could rest easy until at least the end of September. He hushed his mother into silence about this news—it was, he proclaimed with a familial phonetic lisp, a 'thecret' for the time being.

Joe Naisbitt had written from his new home in Transport Command to tell him he too had already been scheduled for a forthcoming stint in Burma. Considering their options like so many other young couples, he and his fiancée had decided to get married before his departure. It seemed like the obvious thing to do, with marriage bringing not only an opportunity to be together for a short while before he left, but also providing his soon-to-be wife with the security and financial benefits that come with being married to an RAF Officer.

Olive's relief at the news of Burma's postponement was followed by a sense of foreboding when she read of Joe N.'s forthcoming nuptials. As the latest letter continued, paragraph by paragraph threw her into a state of absolute and inexplicable desolation. Clearly contemplating Joe Naisbitt's thought process and his own prospect of a long stint away from England on overseas combat, Mac had declared that he wanted to marry Jean early. While she could read his words, she could not take them in. Unable to concentrate long enough to consider the situation from his perspective, she leapt to the assumption that he was trying to punish her in some way with his selfish impulsiveness.

For the first time since Joseph senior had passed away, Olive wept. She should have taken some time to let the emotions pass, but instead she began to write. Flushed with anger, she told her son to stop being foolish. He was far too young to tie himself to another human being for the rest of his life, and he and Jean barely knew each other at all. They had no money, no home of their own or prospect of acquiring one, nothing put aside with which to furnish it, and as her mind raced ahead of her, she sprinted to the inevitable and irrational motherly conclusion that Jean must be rushing him into it.

By the time she calmed down, her notepaper was stained with the salt of her tears, but she did nothing to hide it. Was it the prospective loss of her eldest boy to another woman that was so utterly disillusioning, or was it her intense love and concern for her son to make the best of his yet-to-be-lived life? She knew it was primarily the latter, but there was a primitive instinct making her pen move across the paper now, and the words were sharp and unconstrained. She was, she described, bitterly disappointed in him for being pushed into such a mistake. She posted the letter and went to see Joyce.

It was now July. The light nights and her daughter's ever-sunny disposition both served as a welcome tonic. She was thrilled to find Joyce completely free of her plaster of Paris sarcophagus, although she was still fastened to the bed. She was never good at hiding her feelings, however, and Joyce could tell that she was upset. Assuming it was due to Joe's prospective posting to Burma, she consoled her mother and offered the kind of naïve reassurance that only a sweet teenage girl could. Olive accepted it in silence. At the time of her visit this week, the hospital was busy. The specialist, Mr. Hendry, had been in, examining Joyce's legs and X-rays and declaring that more 'pull' was required. In spite of this, Joyce was chatty, filling Olive's silences with stories of the two birthday parties that the ward had celebrated that week, staying awake until almost midnight and driving the nursing staff crazy.

They were also enjoying a tour by some VIPs, including the Chief Scout himself, Baron Somers, who asked Joyce's fellow patients if there were any Girl Guides on the ward. Sheepishly raising her hand, Joyce's cheeks had turned a fetching shade of puce as he had approached her for a chat. Olive had found the entire situation most surreal, but it had given her plenty to tell the relatives on her visit later that afternoon.

A quick hop 'over home' to see her mother and Phyl had been very worthwhile, particularly since it gave her a chance to spend an hour with little Judith, who, having been previously so desperately ill, was now pleasingly bouncing with health and mischief. Phyl was also in good health, but Gran was not. Olive's mother looked increasingly pale and helpless each time she visited, and she feared for her longevity. She left with a very welcome promise that she could borrow a husband to remove the Andersen shelter from the back garden. She would be glad to be rid of the eyesore that had lived in the back of the house for what seemed like a lifetime and accepted her sister's help gratefully.

When Joe finally replied to her somewhat dolorous last letter, she felt a pang of regret for her calamitous tone, pinched with a back-note of anger that still marred her vision. Her son's words made her feel terrible. He was apologetic and humble, regretting that he had hurt her and cross with himself for her interpretation of what must have been his poor explanation. He had confided in his mother what he now described as the 'thoughts' that were circling his mind, having intended nothing firm in terms of marriage or rash behaviour. Burma was still only a 50:50 possibility, and marriage was only a plan that he had considered putting into action should he be sent on an overseas tour for a long period, which he fully suspected could be up to two years. A letter, he conjectured, was not the appropriate way to deal with the myriad of possibilities and outcomes running around his head. They could talk about it in depth when he got home, whenever that may next be. Jean was not pressing him into action. Olive was relieved to hear both that the rush was off, and that Joe was still affable.

She learned that he had recently signed up to a gunnery instructor's course, utilising this downtime profitably and relishing the idea of being able to pass on the skills that he had himself mastered. He and two other flight sergeants, one of whom was pal and rear gunner, Ivor, had taken and passed the instructor's examination, which had come at the end of the programme. By August, he should be teaching the art of gunnery to recruits.

He had, he told her, also been recommended for an aircraft recognition instructor's course. He would have to go to Sutton, somewhere in Yorkshire, for a week-long intensive programme of training in order to become an instructor in this second subject, but he was very happy about the prospect. It promised to be tough, as three weeks' work was being crammed into just one, and he was expected to give two lectures and take exams at the end of the week. Still, in for a penny, that was Joe.

Joe's Skipper Harry, Olive also learned, was now taking the opportunity to leave the RAF. A former Police Officer, Harry had a hankering to return to the force, and for the rest of the crew this might have a number of outcomes, none of which were yet clear.

Tension abated, Olive had attempted to resume normal correspondence with her son, hoping that their relationship would be unaffected by her words, and that he would understand the deep impact that a mother's anxieties can have on her behaviour. No letter came for a week, however. A trip to Bad Oldesloe in Germany had gone badly, when they lost an engine about 80 miles from their destination. As they approached the runway, the port inner engine had also gone peculiar, all of which resulted in a five-day grounding while both engines had to be replaced. No mail could get out and they were forbidden from leaving the base, so Olive was kept on tenterhooks.

On return to base, Joe was shocked to receive a tirade of abuse from Aunt Hilda, who had taken offence on her sister's behalf and had let loose on Joe about his intentions to marry and abandon his mother. It seemed Olive had unintentionally started a second argument on this prickly subject, and she knew that Joe was madder than hell from reading Hilda's chastisements.

He was also on short pay for five weeks, and owed a small fortune in Mess subscriptions and for the repair of his battle dress, but there was little he could do about that, other than pay.

Joe took his leave in the middle of July in Liverpool, to be greeted by Jean with a gold signet ring. His birthday had passed by in June, almost unnoticed, but she now had time to present him with his gift. It had been skilfully engraved with his initials 'J.H.T' on the front, and more touchingly yet, the words 'FROM JEAN 1945' were curled around the inside of the gold. He was chuffed to bits with it.

Home
Wed: night.

Dear Joseph,

Congratulations on passing your exams as gunnery instructor, more power to your elbow, up the Thompsons etc!! all of which makes me so very bitterly disappointed with you when you say you are thinking of getting married if you have to go abroad. It was no surprise at all, but I did — & still do — hope you will not. Even if you were rushed into being engaged so soon, I did think you would have enough will of your own not to be rushed into tying yourself up for life at the early age of 20. I should certainly think more of Jean than I do now if she would only wait for you without adding to your responsibility when you go. I have been proud of your progress since you joined R.A.F.

& you have it in you to make
a real good thing of your life
son, but I fail to see how
getting married yet awhile will
help. The very thought that you
neither have money nor the things
to start a home with should be
enough to put you off.
Believe me Joe when I tell you
that it is not at all funny
to be dependant on other people
for a home, I've had some & it
meant much unhappiness.
I think — when you think things
over quietly — you will agree that
I have always tried to advise
you to your benefit & I do
sincerely hope & pray that you
will be advised by me now, &
drop the question for a year
at least when you will both
be older & know each other better.
Its not a big sacrifice when
you are so young & I very much
doubt whether the Jap war will

last that long. Marriage can be beautiful, but it so easily spoiled when you havent a home of your own son, & when you do settle you, I'm sure, will agree thats its worth waiting for.

I cant write more now, I'm too upset, but please think everything over very carefully may God bless you always

Love from
Mother.

x x x x

P.S. forgive the tear marks I cant help it.

15

A Summer of Change

Mac
RAF Chedburgh, 1 August 1945–20 August 1945
RAF Burn, Yorkshire, 20 August 1945–28 September 1945
RAF Dunkeswell, Devon, 29 September 1945–31 October 1945

Joyce, it seemed, was getting a summer holiday from 'school'. She may be not actually have been attending school in the traditional sense, but even in the confines of her entrapment in hospital, the long summer break still applied, although for Joyce it would be just four rather than the normal six weeks. Mac wondered that it might not be such a blessing as Joyce thought, since the school work was probably a useful distraction for his sister and her other long-term roommates at the Woodlands. Her latest letter described her boredom vividly. She was fed up with the awful food. Summer seemed to have introduced the opportunity for a whole new gastronomical 'low' in the form of lettuce crawling with grubs. The rain never seemed to stop either, so the girls were still optimising their time by entertaining themselves at the nurses' expense. Their latest rue was to lay their oral thermometers on the red-hot radiators beside their beds, inducing among the young patients of Ward 4 a feverish epidemic of 100-degree-plus across the board. The light at the end of the tunnel for Joyce was the promise of yet another new bed. This time she would once again be tied down and tipped up with her feet aloft, although she would, they promised, be able to be released for massage and exercises.

While Joyce persevered bravely, Mac was packed off complete with a rotten cold, for a week-long aircraft recognition instructor's course. He passed with an 'A', and although he was pretty pleased to be adding this accolade to his string of qualifications, his pleasure was surpassed when he returned to Chedburgh and was met by the news that the Japanese appeared to have had their 'chips' in the Pacific, as well as by over a dozen letters from Jean. As yet, she had never failed to write to him every single day for the year or so that they had known each other, and he ploughed through them diligently.

On 12 August, 218 Squadron was disbanded. None of the crew knew what was to happen next, but they were certain to be sent in different directions.

Olive's description of the summer activities and the preparations for the VJ Day celebrations were colourful, although she sounded melancholy in the knowledge that Joyce would once more miss the party of a lifetime. Den had been packed off on his annual YMCA holidays and Brian had gone to Aunt Lill's in the Black Country for a change of scene.

Olive had received two unexpected and not necessarily welcome visits from her dead husband's ever-absent and most unpopular relatives. She had seen neither hide nor hair of Rose, Joseph senior's sister, since the funeral, and frankly, she had had no desire to do so. Olive disapproved of and disliked Rose. She had been an unmarried mother, which in Olive's traditional strict Victorian mind had brought unnecessary scandal to the family door, and she had offered precisely zero support to her brother's widow after he had suddenly passed away in 1941, leaving her with four young children to manage alone. As she had been leaving the house to go shopping the previous week, Rose's daughter, Winnie, had suddenly appeared, walking up the Grove. Olive, at first hiding her inner tone of contempt, entertained her dutifully, but left her in no doubt about her feelings. There was no chance, she had told Winnie, that they would have ever met again if Winnie had not made the effort to come to Northfield, as Olive herself was far too proud and stubborn to have come to her. The family owed her and she made sure they knew it. Not two days later, Winnie's brother, Albert, and his wife, Eileen, appeared on the doorstep. He was sporting an MBE ribbon and a book full of stories. Again, Olive opened her home to her husband's family and listened as Albert recounted the incident that had earned him his 'gong' when he had attended a troop train smash in Scarborough as a rescuer. They left on reasonable terms, but Olive doubted that she would hear from them again in the foreseeable future.

Mac had received a letter from Harry that boosted his spirits no end. In it, Harry waxed lyrical about Mac, applauding his skills as a gunner and his attributes as a young man and good friend. He could not have felt prouder. His chest was puffed up like a peacock, so moved was he by Harry's kind and effusive words.

However, by VJ Day, Mac had been formally made redundant. He learnt that he would be posted to RAF Burn, near Selby in North Yorkshire, although it was not clear exactly what he would be doing once he got there. The squadron would be posted in batches and Mac would be in the first wave.

As he collected together the kit that he was required to hand back, he was taken aback by how attached he had now become to the tools of his trade. He had no idea just how emotional this simple act would be until the moment he came to do it. His flying gear was handed in first, followed a day later by his small armoury of eight weapons. After such a long attachment and weeks of speculating and talking about the end, it now seemed to have come abruptly and Mac was struggling to wrap his mind around the hard fact that the war was all actually over, or at least only hours away from being so.

VJ Day was dull for Mac but exciting for his sister. She was woken early and the ward was full of singing. They celebrated with a water fight and the first fireworks that Joyce had seen in four years. She now had 'extensions' on her legs, which were essentially just long, wide strips of sticking plaster tape with which the nurses gave her hairy little legs an involuntary 'waxing' at regular intervals when the tapes needed changing. The awful weather dampened no one's spirits.

Mac travelled to his new home in Yorkshire with pal, 'Bish'. They took turns driving Bish's motorbike on the 187-mile journey, taking four hours and thirty minutes, and both bottoms were numb by the time they arrived. The proposed stay at Burn was to be three to four weeks and it looked like a decent place, with good food and decent billets. They had been advised by the powers-that-be that they would work here until such a time as their futures could be decided. A trip before the board would help them unravel in which direction each airman would be best placed to take their future, post-war career. Mac did not have strong feelings either way about what came next, but he hated being bored, so hoped he could find some useful employment that would keep him both busy and interested.

In the meantime, as a number of men were sent off to the local bacon factory, Mac and Bish took to the fields for some good old-fashioned farm work. They both quickly found that they rather enjoyed it. In a wartime bid to maximise crop production, the local farmer had sown wheat and barley in the fields around the aerodrome and between the runways. The two friends were now employed driving the tractor that brought in the newly harvested crops.

Mac had received no pay in the week or so since leaving Chedburgh, and half of their farm wages were now also being taken by the government in national insurance contributions, so money was tight in the extreme. He asked Olive to withdraw £1 from his bank account and forward it to him to stem the drought and he was glad he had asked her for it when he received a forty-eight-hour pass, awarded for his hard work on the tractor. Mac hopped on a train to Liverpool, where he gave Jean the nicest shock of her life, and spent a delightful weekend in Liverpool, including an evening with Arthur Askey at the Empire.

Cigarette shortages were everywhere, including Liverpool, and Mac was not enjoying the forced abstinence. The lack of ciggies was compensated for, however, by a very full stomach, courtesy partially of Jean's mum's cooking and partially due to the thoughtfulness of his mother, who had sent half her rations up for Jean's mother to utilise while catering for her son.

As September flew by, the farm work came to an end and the future became a little clearer. On 28 September, Mac was posted to his new squadron at RAF Talbenny in South Wales. Within two days of arriving, however, the squadron was relocated to Devon due to a change in circumstances at Talbenny. Previously a Ferry Command operating base, it was now being handed over to Transport Command. Typical RAF organisation, thought Mac, and he was on his way again.

By 1 October, he was safely installed at RAF Dunkeswell, near the little town of Honiton on the South Devon coast. It was overcrowded but OK, although the town itself was a disappointment, with only one serving cinema and little else to lure him in. He settled in as best he could and before long had bumped in to a number of former 218 Squadron aircrew. With the longest faces he had ever seen, they were at Dunkeswell waiting for aircraft, as they were heading to the Middle East. In spite of the gloom, he could not help wishing that he was going with them. The camaraderie and frenetic activity of his time in 218 Squadron was much missed.

Here he was housed in a hut with three former POWs. They were most excellent blokes, all having spent over two years in German camps, and he could not wish for finer company while they were in Devon. All former aircrew, they were now on ground duties together. Devon might also provide him with an opportunity to visit Harry, he hoped, who was now living in Bideford, about 50 miles away on the north coast, should the opportunity present itself.

His work was now clerical. Not exciting, but the days went pretty quickly, so that was good. Olive was still sending on batches of 'fan mail' letters, as she described it, due to the growing number of envelopes arriving care of the family home with unrecognisable handwriting. Suspecting that Mac was seeing another girl, she dutifully forwarded the mail, without comment, confiding only in Joyce with her suspicions. Mac found this highly entertaining, especially since the unidentified handwriting had come from the unattractive trio of Tom, his former engineer; Ray, the bomb aimer; and Mrs Clarke, Olive's own neighbour.

Olive had taken Brian into town at the beginning of October for his eleventh birthday. She had bought him a book from Hudson's and they had watched with the rest of the crowds as the post-war celebratory procession stretched 3 miles across Birmingham city centre. That same week, Brian had sat his 11+ entrance examination for Kings Norton Grammar School. His sister had successfully done the same when she was eleven years old, and Brian was a bright little bookworm, so Mac felt confident that he would have no problem also gaining entrance to this prestigious school. He felt a rush of pride in his little brother, who he still thought of as the baby of the family. It seemed like five minutes since he had been donning his little shorts to start Infant School, with legs dangling like knots in cotton. He hoped he would pass and wrote to ask when the results would be in.

Joyce, he heard, was still on a bed, awaiting the doctor's visit. Her friend had been freed from her own shackles and had been up and about in the ward for a few days, although it had later been agreed that her release had been premature, so she had found herself back in bed with the weights reattached. Perhaps, Mac suggested, it was just as well the doctors were taking their time with Joyce then, although he hoped for her sake that she could be home for her birthday at the end of November.

By mid-October, Mac's ex-POW friends had been posted on to other bases, so only he and Bish remained. It had rained so much, incessantly for the last three days, that the camp was a total bog. It was miserable, and Mac was not finding it easy to make new pals here. One of the reasons for this was the fact that the incumbent NCOs at 'Donkey's Well', as Dunkeswell was affectionately known, were mainly sergeants, and for some reason, not quick to mix with the aircrew who tended to be mainly flight sergeants by rank.

He had done a fair bit of flying since arriving here, which he was pleased about, although one trip with a mentally unstable WAAF had forced a one-engined landing at Silworth in Scotland, where he had been obliged to stay for a whole weekend while the engines were fixed.

By the end of October, he heard that Joyce was untethered. The specialist, Doctor Hendry, advised her that her hip, according to the latest X-rays, was now 'consolidated' and she was able to lie freely in bed without any weights or ties. She had been strapped and stretched for more than six months in total and it was a joy to be released. In celebration, she and the other inmates had planned and executed a midnight feast. She wrote to Mac about the full extent of the glory of the occasion. Salads, fish paste and meat sandwiches, biscuits, grapefruit, oranges, apples, pears, chocolate and sweets, fizzy pop and cordial, which was all shared between five girls across their hospital beds. The Night Sister had caught them in the act but seemed to compassionately accept their midnight explanation that it was a 'party', leaving them to get on with it, with reassurances that they would go to sleep after they had finished. Only a tummy ache remained the following morning, but Mac reckoned it must have been worth it and chuckled at Joyce's description of her fear that the Matron might find out what they had been up to. His sister had scattered her letter with hundreds of pencil kisses and he could not wait to see her up and about at long last. He hoped for a miracle that he could be on leave and at home when she would finally come out of hospital.

On the cards for Mac, however, was a new job as his current working section had been classified as unnecessary now that the war was over. Where or what that would be was yet to unfold.

c. 17.8.45

CHEO

Tuesday.

Dear Joyce,

Hello ow his how are you? OK. I hope (& able to read this rotten writing!) I never could write well & being only able to use unlined paper at the moment makes it worse.''

Right now it's running cats & dogs! Which isn't surprising I guess being an English summer

Well ducks it looks as if the war is about over now. The result may be though in a matter of hours.

Our Sqdn has been dis-
banded + I (+ the others)
have been put redundant.
We're being sent to a place
in Yorkshire called B.R.N.
What happens to us
there I dont know.
I've turned in all my
flying clothing + my 8
guns. I was sorry to part
with both but still
I guess it had to come
some time like lots of
other things.
I'd got your letters
waiting for me when I
arrived back here.
I passed that course
incidently with an "A".

Well owing to the fact
its late + I'm at Ches
instead of a civilised camp
I cant write a lot this
time so I hope you will
forgive my brevity.
When I shall be coming
on leave again I dont
know but I promise to
spend more time with
you than I did last
time. Till then (or my
next letter) God-bless
+   Keep Smiling

†
† †
x † †
† †   †
† † †

16

Limbo

Joe
RAF Dunkeswell, Devon, 1 November 1945–15 November 1945
15 Postal Course, RAF Kirkham, Preston, Lancs, 16 November 1945–19 December 1945
1 PDC, RAF West Kirby, The Wirral, 30 December 1945–23 January 1946
9 PDC, RAF North Weald, Epping, Essex, 24 January 1946–10 February 1946

The meantime was occupied by a mixture of clerical duties and some more flying, with trips to various 'dromes around the UK, the return journey often thwarted by inclement weather, and a more pleasant flight to Bordeaux. Here, Mac stayed and awaited the return of his kite, which had gone on to Cairo. Classified as intelligence personnel on this trip, he was not allowed off the camp to look around Bordeaux, but what he could see of the city was in a pretty bad state. It had clearly been severely knocked about by the advancing US troops in the final stages of the war. The sadness that Mac felt had little to do with the destruction itself, which had been a necessary part of getting the job done, but more to do with the regrettable mess that they had left in their wake in a once-beautiful place.

When he returned to Devon, a letter was waiting for him with unfamiliar handwriting. To his delight, it was from Ivor, who had big news. Not only was he to be posted overseas, but, like Joe Naisbitt, he had also chosen to use the hiatus before his departure to get married. Mac could not help wondering whether Ivor's parents had given him the same kind of merry hell for this decision as Olive had given him, but an ironic smirk turned into a larger grin as he read that Ivor was asking him to be his best man. The wedding was to be on 3 November, but it was only days away. Bitterly disappointed, he knew that he would have to decline as he would be unable to get away, much as he wanted the job, since it would be excellent practice for when the time came to marry Jean. He sent a telegram to Ivor straight away with both his apologies and his congratulations in equal measure.

Life went on, mundanely, throughout the remainder of November, and he assumed that Ivor's nuptials went off okay. The 10th was his own anniversary with

Jean—one whole year had passed since their engagement had become official. He was able to swing a weekend's leave, which he took in Liverpool. An additional and unexpected forty-eight-hour pass arrived on Jean's parents' doormat on the Saturday night. Quite how or why it had been sent to Liverpool he had no idea, but, mystery or not, it was nonetheless welcome. The extra time with his fiancée was precious and they took in Abbott and Costello's latest romp before he had to head back to Donkey's Well.

An epic fifteen-hour trip back to the station left him without sleep, and was followed the very next day by an unexpected and ridiculous fifteen-and-a-half-hour journey virtually all the way back from whence he had just come. The destination was Preston, specifically the School of Armaments Training at RAF Kirkham. He was not here to learn about weapons, however, but to learn how to manage an RAF Post Office. Along with some general administrative tuition and accounting methodologies, he had been sent to spend three weeks familiarising himself with the arts of the GPO. Previously an extensive four-month training programme, this course, like so many others in the RAF, had now been condensed and intensified for Mac's enjoyment. On the plus side, he was now only an hour away from Jean, and any new skill was a good skill.

The camp at Kirkham was rubbish, but Mac applied himself to the course as best he could. His thoughts often still turned to home and he now regularly wondered about Joyce and her prospective homecoming. He had heard it was to be soon, if not imminent and he contemplated how it would feel for his little sister to finally walk again after spending such a considerable period incapacitated. Her birthday was coming up at the end of the month and he knew what a treat it would be for both her and his mother to have her home to celebrate. If not for her birthday, then surely for Christmas.

Olive put an end to his speculation as Joyce's birthday came and went without change. Her expected discharge from the Woodlands, she told him, had been a little premature, but she had indeed seen in her fourteenth birthday in an upright position. Although it was an exaggeration to say that Joyce had 'walked', she had certainly had a go. Mac was thrilled for his sister but knew there was a long way to go for her until she would be fully mobile again.

He was expecting to be home on leave once the course was finished around mid-December, and if he and Joyce played their cards right they might finally get to enjoy a Christmas dinner at Olive's table with the full family compliment present.

The postal course was more complex than he had imagined, although it was not exactly intellectually stimulating. There were dozens of daily balance sheets to complete and the vagaries of the Post Office counter to contend with. Wartime restrictions and precautions inevitably overcomplicated the procedures, but he had nonetheless found himself strangely enjoying the work as the days progressed.

Mac was earning £5 every fortnight, minus his income tax, and once it was in his hand he struggled not to blow it all in one outing. Mustering his best Cary Grant impersonation, he joked to Olive, 'Money talks, but all it says to me is "Goodbye."' Another thirty-six hours' leave with Jean proved that to be true to a fault.

Exams, as always, crept up at the end of the course—nine in total—each requiring an in-depth 'swot' beforehand, with accounts proving the most tricky of the bunch for Mac. He considered, as he walked away from the final examination session, that his two years' service anniversary was just around the corner. He really had not done too badly in that time, he realised. At the ripe old age of twenty, he was already a flight sergeant with twenty-two successfully completed operational missions under his belt, and 400 flying hours credited to his name. He reckoned up with a quick mental tally that those hours equated to maybe 80,000 miles in the air. Enough experience to fill a book, he mused. What would the next two years now bring?

A two-week-old letter from Harry arrived, forwarded on from home, and Mac almost fell off his chair when he read its contents. His former skipper and the most excellent of fellows, Harry Warwick, had been awarded the DFC (Distinguished Flying Cross). Gushing with filial pride and reeling from the shock of it, he read and reread Harry's letter, just to be sure of its validity. No one deserved it more and he immediately wrote and told Harry so.

As Christmas approached, Mac learned that he had once more successfully navigated his way through his end-of-course exams and was a qualified postal officer. His leave came through just in time to visit Jean and to return home, fiancée in tow, for Christmas. Jean's parents spoiled him before they left for Birmingham, as always, weighing him down with 100 Senior Service cigarettes and a bag full of other treats for Olive's table. Jean presented him with a smashing canvas-and-leather washbag and it proved to be a very merry Christmas at both ends of the journey. Olive predictably laid on an incredible spread for them all, but by far the most satisfying present was being greeted at the front door by a very tall and skinny Joyce, upright and beaming.

By the end of December, Devon had been exchanged as a base for West Kirby, fortuitously positioned on the Wirral near Liverpool. No. 1 PDC (Personnel Despatch Centre) was a holding base for aircrew destined for overseas postings. As usual Mac had little information about the duration of his stay there, which he was told could be as little as a few days or as long as a few weeks. All roads currently seemed to be pointing toward the Middle East for Mac, but no firm news was yet forthcoming.

Mate Griff was good company as he whiled away the time doing next to nothing all day and planning to visit Jean in the evenings, when he could. Thankfully, they were allowed off the base every evening after 5.30 p.m, as long as they returned, Cinderella-like, by the stroke of midnight. At the first available opportunity Mac walked the 3 miles of country lanes to the nearest train station and, as anticipated, shocked the life out of his fiancée, who had answered the door to find Mac grinning and holding out his arms in a showbiz-like gesture of 'Ta-Da!'

Mac received his draft number the second week in January and with it a slight change of address with a movement from 3 Wing to 2 Wing, but remaining at West

Kirby. He was informed that he should expect to be sent to SEAC (South East Asia Command), but instructions were vague other than that. Mac did not really feel strongly about where he ended up; his interest in exploring and experiencing a foreign country was strong, but his concerns about leaving Jean and his family so far away were real. While he was used to living apart from his loved ones these days, he was not used to being thousands of miles away, so it would be a learning curve for them all.

As January 1946 ended, so did Mac's proximity to Jean. He was relocated to 9 PDC at RAF North Weald, which was located in the middle of Epping Forest in Essex, along with pal Griff. Ostensibly, this was the place where they would wait until they were flown out to India. Not only had they now received instructions regarding the intended country of their destination, but also specifically the name of the place they were headed, which was Maurapur, close to Karachi. Mac knew that the RAF was currently in a state of turmoil in India and Southeast Asia as the news was full of it, so he was not exactly excited at the prospect of being sent into the thick of it all. Strikes were plaguing the RAF stations in the Far East as the tired and war-worn personnel who were awaiting demobilisation grew increasingly cheesed off with the snail-like pace of the action. Relative to the other Armed Forces, it seemed to be taking an age, and the striking, albeit peaceful, was spreading in such a way that it could almost be considered a mutiny. The strikes had begun in Karachi but now involved tens of thousands of men right across Southeast Asia in sixty different RAF stations.

While waiting at North Weald, Mac received his vaccinations in readiness for his new adventure overseas. They had warned him that he may get some kind of a fever following the injections, but he seriously underestimated just how badly they would affect him. He finally gave up and went to see the doctor when his temperature reached 103 degrees. He spent no less than six days 'in the dock' feeling abysmal and wondering what had hit him, before he eventually felt up to getting back to the daily grind.

On 7 February, Mac was woken at 2.40 a.m. and told to ready himself for sailing. An hour later, the whole thing was scrubbed and Mac went back to bed. Mac knew he should be used to the ever-changing plans of the RAF by now, but so specific had been the details concerning his new location in India that he had felt confident that they had finally cemented his future for the next year or two. He was quite wrong. Three days of waiting followed until on 10 February 1946, he was finally put on a ship, but not to India. He was heading to Singapore, where it was intended that he put into practice his newly acquired skills as a postal officer.

By 16 February, he was off the boat and back on *terra firma*, firmly ensconced in his new digs at 6 BPU (British Postal Unit), Singapore.

KIRKHAM.

Monday.

Dear Mom,

Hello "duck". How's life? A bit brighter for you now I'll bet, especially now you've seen the improvement in Joyce & have a good idea when she'll be out. I was very pleased to see that bit of news in both of your letters. I got one last Tuesday & one today with the parcel. I'll bet your wondering why I did not write last week. Well all thro' the week were

had our exams & still
have some to do today.
Fortunately todays will
be the last.
So far we've taken 9
exams & every one
has needed all hell of
a "swot" the night before.
The accounts exams
were the worst, at
least, I think so. I
don't know how I've
gone on in any of
them but will soon
know.
I can't tell you how
relieved I was to get
the parcel today. We've
got a kit inspector

tonight as they've
arrived just in time.
I hope it did not
cause you too much
trouble, 'cos if I
remember rightly the
majority of the kit was
beneath a pile of
letters & things in
that kit bag. Thanks
again all the same.
I hope to be coming
home on leave on
the 13th as I said
before. Just how long I
will get I don't know
but any leave will do!
Somehow I feel as
though I've had no leave

for ages! I cant really
grumble about leave, as
I've had pretty well
in the last 2 years.
Thinking back you know,
I dont think I've
done so bad for less
than two years service
I'm 20, a T/Sgt, I've
got 22 ops to my
credit and 400 hours
flying in; representing
around 80,000 miles.
On top of which I've
had enough experiences
to fill a book, have
visited 4 country's
other than "G.B."
Whilst in a remainising

mood, heres a bit of gen
I got.

That letter you forwarded
on for me was from
Harry (I wish you'd
told me you'd sent it
as its been hanging
about two weeks)
Anyway in it he says
that the weekend he's
writing he received
word that he's been
awarded the D.F.C. !!
Oh! boy was I proud!
I can't get me 'at on !!
Well I guess thats
about all the news
for now. If I don't
write again I'll see

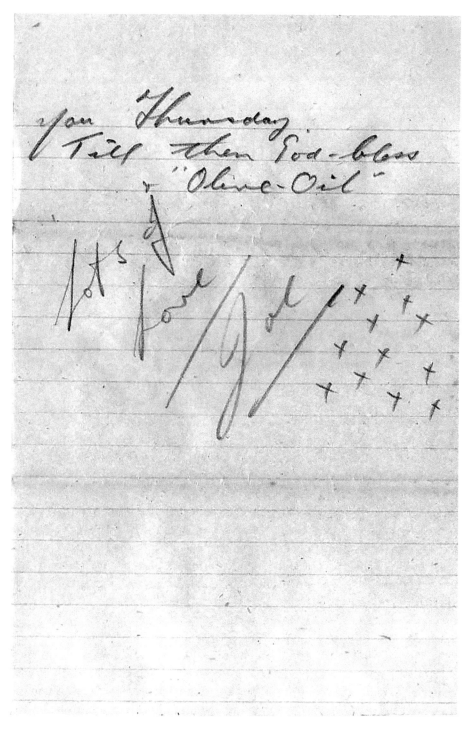

17

A Posting Overseas

Olive
Northfield, Birmingham
16 February 1946–8 February 1947

Olive had heard nothing from her son for weeks and while she no longer wore the same cloak of worry that she had during his days of combat, she could not help but wonder why no letter had arrived either for her or for Jean since Christmas. The irony that Joe was now in charge of a post office was not lost on her, of course.

They had endured a few difficult months at home in the lead up to Christmas. While the end of the fighting had been joyous, Olive had had to deal with the long absence of Joyce and her deep concerns about her only daughter's hospitalisation. She thanked God that the girl was now home, although she had been barely able to walk over the festive period. Receiving the news that Joyce would finally be allowed out of hospital had been such a boon, although Olive had had to force the hand of the consultant who had been reluctant to release Joyce in time for Christmas. In preparation for the big homecoming, Olive had prepared a bag of things, which included Joyce's best dress and coat to travel in, and had gone to the Woodlands to meet her. It had taken them both by surprise when Joyce had changed into her dress and stood up to find that all the stretching on the 'rack' had resulted in several inches of growth, in turn rendered her skirt length embarrassingly short. With little alternative option and a brace face, Joyce had travelled back home in it, tugging at the hem and drawing her coat in around her to preserve her dignity.

In addition to the situation with Joyce, Olive had had to break the news to the children that her own sister, Violet, had sadly passed away. They had distracted each other with tasks around the house, and Olive had employed the children in gathering together the remnants of Joe's kit, which had been scattered around the house, urgently required by Joe for an inspection. Although the news that he had been due to be posted overseas had not been entirely unexpected, her heart had sunk with the knowledge that his absence was likely to be prolonged. She wondered how Jean would cope without his regular presence in Liverpool, too.

Hilda, so terminally unlucky, had also been suffering as the result of a miscarriage, and Olive was carrying her burden in addition to her own, as was her way. She visited when she could but Joyce's mobility was so poor when she first came home that there was little question of her dragging the girl halfway across Birmingham.

January had brought better news, but with it, terrible weather. Joyce's knee pain, quite severe when she had begun putting her weight on it, was now easing and her movement was considerably improving as a result. She had even played a game of football in the street with Brian and another pal, albeit a severely lacklustre one.

It had been bitterly cold and there had been significant snowfall in recent weeks. It snowed on and off for the best part of a month, and by mid-February, the whole country appeared to be crippled. The weather was only partly to blame for the nation's problems, however, which were affecting people near and far, or so the radio suggested. As far as Olive could see, the country was trapped in a vicious downward spiral of bitter temperatures, lack of coal, wide unemployment, and little food everywhere. Rations, or the lack of, were worse now than at any point she could remember during the course of the war years. At the heart of the problem were coal shortages, which had become so catastrophic nationwide that it had resulted in almost 2 million people becoming unemployed. The fuel shortages had shut down industry, including the huge local Cadbury factory and the Austin, where almost 9,000 workers now lay idle. Olive's was one of the only departments that was still operating, but the conditions were so bad that she had to work wearing her enormous ARP overcoat and gloves, just to keep from freezing. Once daylight faded, which was early, given that they were in the depths of winter, the lack of electricity made it impossible to work, so they were forced to pack up and go home for the day.

As far as domestic electricity was concerned, things were no better. The government had now imposed a forced power outage for five hours every day in order to try to conserve coal, which the miners were unable to produce quickly enough. Even if the coal had been available, the rampant snow had brought the railways to a complete halt, making its distribution impossible.

While Olive knew that the Austin bosses had paid their redundant workers for the first two weeks in which they were laid off, they were then forced onto the dole. She was now struggling more than ever to keep the house warm and to feed her hungry and growing family. With Joe in Singapore, unable to help, she could only do her best. So dire were the current shortages that she had even been forced to queue for potatoes, but thankfully, to date, their coal supply was still being delivered, even if they were down to just three bags per month, barely adequate in the relentless bitterness of this winter.

The nibs, immune as always from the politics of the situation, had taken advantage of the snow in the usual fashion. They had sledged and sledged until they were wet through and as cold as ice. In some areas, the snow was so bad that drifts had covered double decker buses, but the kids cared not a hoot as they had the time of their lives outdoors.

Soldiering on was now an inherent part of Olive's make-up, and she continued to persevere with the limited frugal supplies she did have. A large envelope arrived addressed to Joseph, which in the absence of a line of communication with her son, she opened. Inside was Joe's Gratuity Book, containing £53.18.0. She had understood that these funds were usually given out once a serviceman had been demobbed, so was curious as to whether it had actually been sent in error, since Joe's demob was not yet in sight. She decided to sit on it for Joe until he could sort out the facts for himself and she wrote to advise him that he was potentially in the pink.

Phyl had written to Olive to tell her that poor Gran, such a worry at the best of times these days, had now had a nasty fall in the snow, badly bruising herself and breaking a finger. Thankfully it had been no worse than superficial injuries, but Olive knew that her mother was on a downward decline and that she must brace herself for the worst in the not too distant future.

It was still snowing on and off during the last week of February and Olive recognised that she was the only person in the Grove who was leaving the house each morning to go to work, such was the extent of the impact of the situation on people's employment. She spent each and every lunchbreak on the hunt for food, trotting between local shops looking for potatoes and other short supplies. She was royally fed up with making things stretch and, like most of the nation's housewives, was shocked by the continued need to 'make do' so many months after the end of the war.

Joyce finally received the all-clear to return to school, although Olive was nervous about the slippery conditions that her daughter would need to navigate. The very last thing she needed was for Joyce to fall on the ice and dislodge her hip, undoing all the good work that had been put in during all those months in hospital.

As February drew to a close, the snow began to thaw, bringing with it a new problem in the shape of localised flooding, which destroyed the much-needed wheat and potato crops. It was a depressing situation.

News finally came from Joe who, by the first week of March, still appeared to be in India, awaiting onward transfer to Singapore. The heat, he had proclaimed, although so hot that he could barely breathe, was not as bad as they had been told to expect once they reached Singapore, which would be more humid and oppressive. Joe had been joined in India by two of his buddies, Jack Griffin and Ron Barnes, both of whom coincidentally seemed to be destined for the same Postal Unit as Joe in Singapore. They had been filling the days so far getting orientated, playing tennis and doing their level best to hide the distaste that they felt for the smelly and squalid conditions in which the locals lived. He had managed to acquire a pillow for himself for the grand sum of '2 chips', only to discover that they had to carry their own bedding around everywhere when they moved, which had been more frequent than he might have liked.

Their arrival in India had been via RAF Poona where they had stayed for one night, then RAF Arkonam, and on to their current lodgings at RAF Tambaram, No.

209 Staging Post, all via epic train journeys. Joe was getting used to the currency of rupees and annas, and by the time he arrived at Tambaram, he was familiar with the price of every conceivable variety of fruit, as well as the necessary packet of Players ciggies, from the frequent stops at roadside sellers. He had scanned the local shops and markets with wonder, but alas no funds. He had considered what a marvellous pair of shoes he could buy for Jean or Olive if he had 25 rupees to spare, which would cost the earth at home. Bananas and monkey nuts were all he could afford right now, however, as he had not been paid.

He eked out his funds and his time until the very end of March, when the boat finally left India for Singapore. He arrived on the 26th at his new home, which was in a fairly upmarket looking department. He was to share a room with Griff in the 'Amber Mansions', which every inch lived up to its promising name. Now they were making another conversion from rupees, to dollars and cents, and while the adjustment took no time at all, it quickly became apparent that their newly discovered skill at negotiating on price might as well have been left behind with the rupees.

Everything in Singapore was plentiful but, alas, expensive. Having forked out a hefty $6 for two films for the small camera that he had borrowed from Jean, Joe had been quick to reset Olive and Jean's expectations about what treats he might be sending home.

Singapore immediately fascinated Joe. The mixture of races here was wide. There were 'Straits' Boys, Chinese, Cantonese, and a sprinkling of Tamil Indians were also mixed in with the Malay majority. Their billet had a 'bearer boy', which appeared to Joe to be another name for a servant. They would pay him $2 per week to work for them as chief bed-maker, tea-bringer, laundry-sorter, shoe-polisher, and general clean-and-tidier. Joe was more than happy to fork out for such excellent help and wondered how the boy managed to survive on a wage that was probably around a fifth of what he would need to earn himself to live here.

In Singapore, the weather, like the RAF, seemed to have its own routine. It would start to rain every day at around 12 p.m. to 1 p.m. and last for a predictable two hours before stopping as suddenly as it had started. Joe had never seen rain like it, to say nothing of the thunder and lightning. Although each daily soaking brought cool relief from the soaring temperatures, once it ended, it left behind a stifling, damp humidity, which strangled their lungs.

Singapore was a huge, modern metropolis, with a large number of cinemas, theatres, servicemen's clubs, and other halls of entertainment. Best of all, there were a total of ten public swimming pools, the best and most modern of which was reserved for forces personnel only. If that were not draw enough for her son, Olive knew that the fact it served up excellent grub would have hit his jackpot.

They received a letter from Joe in April and they could see from the enclosed snaps that Joe's suntan was deepening quickly. As far as Olive's maternal eyes could tell, however, he looked emaciated, his ribs clearly visible beneath the skin of chest in the tiny black and white photos. He seemed to spend a great deal of time, or so Joyce surmised, walking about semi-naked in a kind of adult nappy. Perhaps, she had quipped to Olive, they should send him a safety pin? Joyce and Brian had both written marvellous letters for their big brother, explaining the terrible food shortages back home and including a few cracks about sweating and smelly feet. Joe must have been shocked to hear about the rationing, as within a couple of weeks a parcel of tinned food arrived, much to everyone's delight, along with a copy of the RAF's Singapore newspaper for a little light reading.

Joe had discovered that the food situation in Singapore, while not as scarce as back in Blighty, was a lot more hazardous for one's health. Olive heard that, along with a dozen other men, he had been 'in the dock' with food poisoning for five days. Horrendous stomach cramps and vomiting had floored them all and some were blaming the awful dehydrated food, others the beer rations, but it had eventually been traced back to tinned dehydrated onions, which he swore to steer clear of from that moment on.

His work in the sorting section, of which he was in charge at the BPU, was going well. Dealing with all incoming mail from the UK, he was responsible for letters and packages destined for all parts of the SEAC, including Burma, Malaya, Borneo, Java, Sumatra, Siam, China, Japan, and French Indochina. Griff, Joe's roommate was in charge of all the mail going in the opposite direction, and staff shortages meant that Griff had a hell of a job keeping up. More kites and extra bodies were promised, however, to prevent the backlogs from worsening. They worked in shifts—8 a.m. to 4 p.m., 4 p.m. to 12 a.m., and 12 a.m. to 8 a.m. It was relentless and tiring work, but it made the time fly.

Back home, to Olive's great relief, Joyce had returned to school and appeared to be coping well, relishing it in fact. Every day brought an improvement in her walk and she was now riding her clapped out old bicycle, much to Olive's disdain. She had asked Den to do a check on the brakes and its general road safety, which had eased her mind somewhat. He was becoming a real man about the house these days. He had cleaned out the coal shed located in the alleyway fondly known as the 'entry', between number 16 and 14, and was currently in the process of converting it into a store for his tools. Now a bona fide painter and decorator, he had accumulated a good deal of paraphernalia, which he needed to keep in a safe place that was not under Olive's feet. She had decided to maximise his availability as a live-in tradesman and was currently employing him in redecorating the bathroom in what she considered to be a classy black and cream colour scheme. The children had pulled a number of faces when she had revealed her monochrome plans, including feigned vomiting and utter confusion, but she was sticking to her guns.

As if in acknowledgement that 1946 would be a better year, the large apple tree in the back garden was now in full blossom. It had been full of equal promise in previous years, of course, but the fruit had steadfastly and resolutely refused to appear. She hoped more than ever for a harvest this year, with the food situation being as it was. It was now late April and the garden was looking alive at last, thanks to the hard work put in by the nibs and Olive's brothers-in-law.

The anniversary of Joseph senior' death did not pass unnoticed by either Olive at home or by Joe in Singapore. Olive sorely missed having both of them around, their long limbs in front of the hearth and their help with the hard labour around the place.

Joe's most recent letter informed her that Group 40 and Group 41 aircrew had now been sent home, demobbed at last. Perhaps the strikes had done the trick, she pondered. In addition, the men of Group 47 were in the middle of their demob medical examinations, so were also likely to be on their way soon enough. Joe seemed optimistic that he would be at Olive's Christmas dinner table himself.

The rainy season had taken its toll on Joe. He was waking each morning to discover that his clothes and shoes were green with mildew and were remaining damp all day long. The ferocious electric storms that came with alarming frequency were fascinating, but the humidity that accompanied them was unbearable. As summer now approached, although the heat was intensifying, the humidity was improving slightly to make life more tolerable, although in its place, prickly heat was now raging among most of the men. Joe found that it penetrated his pores, joking that it was hardly worth taking a drink since a consumed cup of tea or glass of water would return to his skin's surface less than ten minutes later it in the form of burning, itching sweat.

Hunger was never far away for Joe when he was away from his mother's kitchen, and it seemed to Olive that he spent most of his RAF wages on supplementing his meals by buying food elsewhere. The food poisoning, which seemed to be a regular problem in Singapore, had also recently taken hold of thirty-two Chinese workers who had been eating bread. From Joe's description of the Army baked loaves he had been offered, Olive was left unsurprised that it had caused fatalities. It was riddled with weevils and bugs and, according to Joe, a wise man would hold up each morsel to the light before biting into it, to inspect it in a kind of DIY 'X-ray' examination. It was not unknown to find the occasional ant taking refuge in the middle of a mouthful, so caution was advised.

Along with the local newspaper with Joe's handwritten translated annotations, Olive had also received the leaf from a rubber tree and an Occupation $10 bill. The kids had quickly taken possession of the latter precious artefact, which was destined for the school playground where it would be flaunted as a trophy from their familial hero. The currency had been printed and distributed by the Japanese during their occupation but was now worthless, enabling Joe to buy a handful of them in a number of denominations for just 10 cents.

He was enjoying this fascinating place and, were it not for Jean and the family's need for him back home, he would have liked to consider staying on and exploring the many opportunities that would clearly be available for westerners after demobilisation and into the future.

By the end of May, the demob had been speeding up, it seemed. Groups 46 and 47 were now expecting to be going home imminently and it felt as though they had flown through the last seven groups in just a short period of weeks. That must bode well for Joe's Group 57's prospects, Olive pondered. She was folding and sending him Birmingham's weekend newspaper, the *Weekly Post*, as regularly as possible, since he had declared himself to be news-less. With no radio to listen to and the prospect of purchasing one unlikely, since they were priced well out of Joe's range at around $300 apiece, she knew he would relish some local stories and the news of his beloved Birmingham City's football results. She was learning that it was a lot faster to send anything small enough to be bundled into an envelope with a 2½d stamp to Joe via normal mail, rather than as a package. Thanks to her son's insider knowledge of the postal system, she now knew that the former would be conveyed by air, whereas all other mail was transported by boat, taking weeks to reach its destination.

She was also learning that her son had resourcefully found effective mother-substitutes in Singapore for the majority of the domestic tasks with which he needed help. '*Dhobi*' meant laundry and there was never any need to hang out the washing for more than half an hour, he told her, such was the ferocity of the heat. Although there was a laundry service on offer, it had a maximum tolerance of twelve items that could be sent for washing per week, so Joe was unable to escape the task altogether. As far as repairs to uniform went, the local 'sew-sew' women could be hired for just a few cents to alter or repair any item of clothing in super-fast time. They even came calling door-to-door two or three times per day, negating the need for Joe to seek them out. It was a quality service, that was for sure.

Joe's twenty-first birthday was approaching, and Olive set about writing to him, enclosing £1 for him to spend on himself. Feeling his absence keenly, she took the time to tell him just how proud she felt of his progress and attitude since he had left the family home to join the RAF. He was now a man and she could hardly believe that her eldest was about to come of age. How life had changed them all these past few years. Olive could never have imagined at the start of the war that she would be here now, husbandless, with a son in the Far East. He deserved success and she ensured that she told him so in this most special of birthday letters.

Brian was sat with his nose stuck in his growing stamp collection. He could spend hours sorting, sticking, and examining the little paper treasures and he now lifted his head to ask Olive whether she thought Joe would be able to supply any interesting additions to his collection. She told him she would be sure to ask, since if anyone had access to a decent selection of foreign stamps, it would surely be a post master. One thing she did know was that a holiday was overdue for all of them. Although Den would probably have to stay home and work, Olive was plotting a nice break for her and the two nibs in Blackpool for a few days. They were all ready for it.

By the end of June, Groups 46 and 47 were no closer to their promised demob than they had been at the start of May when the carrot had originally been dangled in front of them, so Olive was still left clueless as to when she could expect her son home. He had declared that Group 46 had now been told that it would be August or September at the earliest before they would leave for the UK, so it was unlikely to be this side of 1947 for Joe's lot.

Olive received word from Jean that she would like to come for a visit, and she had asked whether it would be okay if she brought her younger sister, Mary, along too, for a little break. Olive had been happy to oblige, knowing that Mary, albeit a shy girl, would be excellent company for Brian and Joyce. She was planning, as always, to feed them fit to burst, even though bread had now been added to the ration list, and to send them home feeling as though they had been closer to Joe.

As far as his own stomach was concerned, it was now apparently costing Joe $20 per fortnight to fill. Resentfully, Joe was venturing in to town on a daily basis to supplement the wholly inadequate meals that the RAF were providing, the latter of which lacked in both quantity and quality.

Jean and Mary spent an excellent weekend with Olive. Jean was sporting a fine pair of handmade leather shoes, which Joyce had immediately lusted after. It seemed they had been custom made to order in Singapore, courtesy of Joe, who had now also offered to get both Joyce and Olive a pair each. Following his instructions, they had giggled furiously while each stood on a piece of brown paper in stockinged feet as the other used a pencil to draw a pattern of the size and shape of each of their feet so that Joe could get them correctly sized to fit. Joyce's feet were so ticklish that the slightest movement of the pencil sent her into raptures of hysteria, and they had all enjoyed the moment while it lasted, knowing that it also attached each one of them to Joe via an invisible cord.

Joe, meanwhile, was not only fed up with the interminable wait for demob, but had now also learned that he was to lose rank. All warrant officers and flight sergeants were to be reduced in rank to sergeant, while retaining the higher-level pay. He had recently also declared his intentions to leave the RAF. While he was getting much enjoyment from exploring the Far East, and heat rash aside, he found the RAF to be increasingly a hot-bed of red tape and bureaucracy and he had no appetite for it whatsoever during peacetime.

News from Joe via his letters was still very few and far between, the latest correspondence having taken eight weeks to reach them, judging by the date he had handwritten on it. Such was the state of the backlogs of mail that he now had twenty Japanese POWs helping out, hauling mail bags and attempting to move the vast amount of mail that stood idle, waiting for its journey home.

The summer holidays had brought awful weather in the UK, but Joyce and Brian had, as usual, made the best of it and had thoroughly enjoyed the short trip to Blackpool. The persistent rain had been so bad that, as they travelled home, Olive could see how it had blackened fields of wheat, leading her to the conclusion that there was unlikely to be an end to the bread rationing any time soon.

When the holidays ended, the kids prepared to go back to school. For Joyce, good news came in the form a declaration by her specialist that her hip was 'marvellous'.

For Brian, excitement had been building since the excellent news that he had passed his 11+ exam and had gained entry to the prestigious boys' Grammar School at Kings Norton. A new phase of his little life was marked with the purchase of his new uniform. Olive had spent what felt like a small fortune on the required uniform and other accoutrements, as well as new school shoes for the ever-bigger Joyce.

If this had not left her short enough financially, she had also been docked two days' work by the factory bosses the previous week as she had been caught trying to 'escape' before 12.30 p.m. She had been among a dozen others who had all received similar punishment for the same crime. The free time had been used to go and see the doctor, but the pay was missed. Although she had made light of it in front of the children, she had been becoming increasingly concerned about a problem with her arm, which had begun a few weeks ago and was leaving her with nerve pain and numbness on one side, all the way down to her fingertips. The doctor's visit had been only semi-fruitful, in that he had not been entirely sure of the cause, but had suggested a series of treatments. She lived in hope.

As the weeks flew by with little word from Joe, she found him more and more regularly in her thoughts. On Sunday evenings, his absence was particularly obvious as she parcelled up the weekend newspapers and wrote a few lines of simple news. Each week, she knew, although a symbol of his lengthening absence, could only be bringing his homecoming closer and closer.

By late autumn 1946, the lack of news from Joe's end was worrying Olive to such an extent that she decided to take matters in to her own hands. She wrote a letter that she addressed and mailed directly to the CO in Singapore, in the vain hope that his personal mail would be treated with a greater degree of urgency than the norm and that he would be able to shed some light for her upon the drought in communications with her son, for whose welfare she was becoming increasingly concerned. The CO certainly received her letter. A flushed Joe was summoned immediately to see him, causing him palpitations with the anticipation that something terrible might have occurred back home. His worry turned to embarrassed relief when he discovered the cause of the CO's demand for his presence, and a telegram was immediately dispatched to his mother to reassure her that he was indeed alive and well.

Olive had grown accustomed to the wishing and hoping, which now accompanied the ritual of signing and sealing each of the love-filled letters she wrote to her boy. He would be home soon, she remembered. Patient waiting, Olive hoped, would be eventually rewarded with the feeling of him back in her arms.

11ᵗʰ/6/46

Dear Mom,

Well it's me again. Today
I recieved youre birthday letter
+ present to me. Bless you and
thanks mom. I hope I can live
up to the nice things you said
in it. I shall try my best to
do so.

Really you should not have
sent that pound, not that I
don't appreciate it, but because
I know how every penny you
have + always have had, has
to go a hell of a long way.
Thank God I've such a mother as
you.

I see that you are all set up
for a holiday. Good show, you
surely deserve it Joyce too. I only
wish I could be with you but
as I can't it does not stop me
from saying I hope you all

have a wizard time, wizard weather a good pile of fun & rest. You need it. Our kid I see is doing the lone pioneer this year. Independance is a good thing! I'm still plagued by this B—— prickly heat! Drives yer nuts! Just like a thousand pen nibs being stuck in you; when I drink a cuppa-tea its blue-murders, 'cos it makes one sweat straight away. Cold water does too!! You drink it at 12 AM & at 12-15 its come out of you again as perspiration!!!

I recieved another bundle of papers yesterday and have read them till my eyes were raw. Jack is now deep in the 'Post learning more of B'ham. Tell Brian I'm not having a great deal of success as far

as stamps for his 1 album is
concerned but have about 20
down at the office (yes, I've got an
office!)

I see that Ivan doesn't improve
yet become any the worse. I
guess that the benefits of a bath
chair will be a help to both
aunt Phyl + Ivan too. Evan could
certainly do with the fresh air.
I've written to 57 incidently.
There's not a lot to write about
here just prickly heat (we've
all got that!) lousy food in the
mess (we've all got that too!!)
+ the slow rate of demob which
we all haven't got yet. To be
quite honest, it doesn't worry
me a lot, all the griping we
do or could do would never
speed it up fully, and anyway
I want to have a look around

this way first!!! Don't think I fancy staying in the Raff; there is enough "Bull" & red-tape as it is without staying in the public peace-time R.A.F. !!!

I hear that from the period 1st of Aug: to Sept: 30th 46 - 47 will be out. Whether that official yet I don't know but if it is then there will be the advancement of 1 group only for aircrew since the last promulgation!! Press-on! Press-on!

Jack gets so lett-up over the demob. he says he'd like to prang the big nob in charge with a beer bottle! Thats an idea anyway!

Well our Olive, I must close for now as its getting late.

Have a bang-on holiday & don't forget to tell me all about it.

Whust go now! Toodle-oo for this time ducks. Thank again for the £1 — (its a change to handle good money!) God-bless.

Lots of love / Joe /

18

The Final Throes

Mac
Ward 16, 47 British Military Hospital, Singapore, 9 February 1947–April 1947
Westminster Hospital, Chelsea, England, April 1947–22 September 1947

Christmas came and went with relentless heat. Mac worked and waited for news of his anticipated journey home, with nothing but a pleasant certainty that he would soon be back at Elmdale in the crisp cold of a Birmingham winter, just as it had been when he had begun his adventure three years earlier.

On Tuesday 4 February 1947, Mac and his associates were finally given the news that they were to go for their Release Medical Examinations. This meant that demob was on the horizon at last. Joe could not have been happier. He had been longing to hold the fiancée that he had missed so much, and to hear the sounds of the nibs' laughter, and he was so close that he could almost taste his mother's home cooking and feel the snow getting inside his boots.

As instructed, he and his fellow workers attended the sick bay at the allotted time for their routine examination which would 'rubber stamp' the end to this incredible military chapter in their lives.

The young men who stood in line with Mac had all faced countless medical exams before this moment and none bore any concerns about the process or the likely outcomes; they were, after all, still very young men, strong and fit to boot. This, ironically, would be a far more thorough examination than the one undertaken when Mac had volunteered for service back in 1943. This was in no way intended to be for the benefit of the servicemen who were subjected to it, however. With thousands of demobs happening all over the world, the authorities were extremely keen to ensure that no one had claim to more disability allowances than were strictly their entitlement. Finances were, after all, tight after the expense of this epic six-year war.

Mac was still without any major worries when the medical officer spent longer than usual on the examination of his private parts. There were stifled smirks from the boys in the queue, who had little reason to doubt that Joe was simply being subjected to over-zealous attention on what was certainly the part of the medical that they always hoped to be hurried through as quickly as possible. For Mac, this was simply embarrassing, nothing more. After a short amount of prodding and questioning, however, the smiling subsided. He was taken aside to a small table, where he was questioned at some excruciating length about the condition of his testes. The medical officer had discovered what appeared to be a small, hard lump sitting just behind Mac's left testicle. Joe had noticed the lump before, but since there was neither pain nor discomfort emanating from the area in question, he had chosen to ignore it. He had almost forgotten its existence, such was his nonchalance, but the medical officer begged to differ and was not willing to allow the finding to pass without further inspection.

Over the next few days, he was sent for further examinations, just to be on the safe side. He visited the sick bay once more for blood tests and waited patiently for the officious male nurse to prepare his equipment and paperwork. It took several frustrating and painful attempts before the nurse finally managed to insert a needle in his arm and extract enough blood for the required tests. A rather irritated and sore Mac was informed that it was unlikely to be anything serious, probably just a benign growth or cyst, which would amount to nothing. He would, however, need to wait for the blood tests before they would be able to tell him any further news.

In the interim period, as instructed, he got back to normal routine, until he received notice to report once again to the sick bay for his test results. For precautionary reasons only, he was told, it was suggested that the growth be removed as swiftly as possible and examined. It was highly unlikely that a twenty-one-year-old man in such excellent physical condition, showing no symptoms of fatigue or pain, would be unfortunate enough to have any sinister conditions, this would be rare in the extreme. Content with this information, Mac resigned himself to the idea that he would get the operation over and done with, have the suspected cyst removed and move on. That way he could continue to his demob with the knowledge that he had a clean bill of health with which to begin the next chapter of his life, having had the issue dealt with quickly and neatly.

As yet, he had told Olive and Jean nothing of these events, fearing that the news would sent them both into a tailspin of panic, but honesty now seemed the best policy. He wrote to his mother explaining cheerfully that, in spite of this small setback, he was in excellent general health and that it should have no bearing on the timelines for his homecoming. He would no doubt be out of Singapore and the RAF by the end of April and on a boat home. She was not, under any circumstances, to worry about his wellbeing. He was fine, and the Japanese-built Alexandra military hospital to which he was to be admitted seemed excellent from what he could see— it was certainly very modern and comfortable.

Mac underwent surgery to remove the offending growth on 15 February 1947. It took weeks for the letter filled with this news to reach Olive's hands. She read the hastily-scrawled lines with her heart in her mouth and a familiar feeling of utter helplessness. Torn between the relief of Joe's assurances that it was nothing serious, the belly-wrench that told her to fly immediately to his side, and the knowledge that she could not, Olive was once again thrust into a world of uncertainty and fear.

Joe's optimism proved premature. The results of the surgery, which he had dismissively assumed would be the end of the matter, concluded that Mac's condition was more serious than anyone had considered, and it became clear that he would not be making his way home with his newly demobbed, civvy-wearing pals in April. The investigatory tests into the apparently harmless testicular tumour had concluded that it was, in fact, malignant. Joseph, at twenty-one years of age, had testicular cancer.

It is impossible to describe the gravity that accompanied the receipt of this savage news by the family back home. For four years, Olive had watched her eldest boy become a man from a distance. He had walked out of her front door at the age of eighteen, as the war had been at its height, and he had thrown himself whole-heartedly into the action. He had survived twenty-two dangerous and often near-death operational sorties deep into enemy territory, under heavy fire, and he had been shot down in the freezing sea in the depth of winter and still made it home to her fireplace. He was within a fingertip's reach of the end of his adventurous journey, with his entire life to live and a young fiancée that he would finally be able to wed, and tragedy had struck her beautiful boy.

It was rare, but knowing that it was unlucky somehow exacerbated the bitter knife-twist in the belly that Olive felt. He did not deserve it, and her head was full of questions, the biggest question of all being the only one that could not be answered. Why it had happened to her son was a mystery that would not be solved.

Joe remained in hospital in Singapore for a further few weeks, recovering from the surgery and undergoing basic treatment. He would have to await a transfer to the UK so that he could be admitted to a hospital with appropriate facilities for his condition. In the meantime, both Olive and Jean had to wait and hope once more.

Joe arrived back in England in the middle of April 1947, but was not allowed home to Birmingham. He was transported immediately to Westminster hospital in Chelsea in order to undergo the most cutting-edge treatment available for cancer of this kind, which would be carried out under the supervision of eminent cancer specialist Mr Stanford Cade.

Ironically, although Joe was now closer to home than he had been for over a year, it was still almost impossible for Olive to visit him. Her work responsibilities kept the family afloat, so from Monday to Saturday she worked and worried, then grasped the only available opportunity to see her son that she could, on Sundays.

Armed with food and gifts, she made the multi-hour, extravagantly expensive train journey from Birmingham to London, usually with Joe's two or three siblings in tow. She loaded up rations, newspapers, books, and baked goods for her son and dragged the brood across the capital as often as she was able, desperate to be with Joe and to aid his swift recovery.

Westminster Hospital was a large, relatively new building, situated in St John's Gardens at the heart of London's affluent and leafy Notting Hill area. The prestigious surgeon and radiotherapy pioneer Stanford Cade was a highly decorated specialist, internationally renowned, having written two books on the treatment of cancer. He had himself worked as a volunteer reserve in the RAF and acted in an advisory capacity on projects and research relating to the improvement of cockpits for pilots, which later won him a knighthood for his work and research. He had already dedicated many years to this field of treatment, but the odds, he knew, were not good. The fatality rate for men with testicular cancer was high and there were as yet no successful chemotherapy practices in common use.

Mr Cade was of Russian descent (born Kadinsky) but had been educated in Europe and was evacuated to England during the First World War. Although already tri-lingual when he reached England, he had spoken no English, but the fact that he pursued a career and studies in the complexities of medicine while simultaneously attempting to learn the language in which he was being instructed left Olive in little doubt about his character and diligence. Joe, it seemed, was in good hands.

Cade became a pioneer in the treatment of malignant disease with radium. It was this, in the form of X-ray therapy, which was to be the main contributor to Joe's treatment.

Joe was cheery but longed to be home. Hospital confinement was incredibly boring, and he still had little doubt that, once the treatment was completed, he would be allowed home to get on with his life. He lived for the family visits, and the letters that he read over and over transported him home. It was impossible not to think about Jean and the marriage plans that they had deferred out of respect for their parents' wishes, for two and a half years. He did not doubt they would marry, for in his mind that was a certainty— not a question of if, but of when. He would have to be patient about his recovery, although the X-ray treatment was tougher than he had expected and he felt grim most of the time. The medical staff were strict, severe, and relatively uncommunicative about his prognosis and they said little or nothing about how long he would have to stay in hospital. He had little choice but to do as he was told, rest, accept the treatment, and wait for the day of his 'release'.

Too much time to think led to the inevitable subjects of marriage and children. He wondered tentatively whether the surgery would have an impact on his ability to have a family. It was not an easy thought process to consider whether Jean would still love him if he could not father the children that she deserved? She would make a phenomenal mother, this he knew already and it made him anxious to consider the alternatives, so he pushed it away and focused on more positive feelings where he could. He was not a pessimistic man by nature, and it was vital to him and, he knew, to Jean and the family that he protect all his loved ones by being cheerful and upbeat in his correspondence.

On painfully few occasions for both of them, Jean was able to come and visit. It was a tortuous journey from Liverpool as well as a struggle for Jean to take the time off work. But when she arrived in the clinical whiteness of the hospital ward, it was like Joe had taken delivery of an enormous bunch of flowers. Her sweet smile and the softness of her hands on his were worth waiting for.

They would talk about Liverpool, their respective families, and Joe's treatment. They made plans for Christmas and a holiday at the seaside but Joe could see that his fiancée was unable to fully relax. He put it down to the situation and the presence of the other patients around them, but there was something in her eyes which looked like sadness, and he wanted with all his heart to extinguish it. He felt completely helpless, not wanting to be here, miles from home, tired and imprisoned. The promise of his own soft mattress and trips to the pub with his newly demobbed mates in the Grove kept his spirits up, but with every visit, both Jean and Olive could see the changes in his body, and in his face when they touched his cheeks.

Visiting hours would pass too quickly and then Jean and her laughter would be gone again. Back to the stern crispness of the nurses and the fatigue, which seemed to be creeping in at the corners a little more each day.

On 24 May 1947, Olive's stress levels peaked when her long-suffering mother, Mary, finally succumbed to her ill health and passed away. It was a terrible time for Olive. Her worries about Joe had to be side-lined for a short time as she dealt with the funeral and her multiple siblings. Joseph was too unwell to attend the funeral. He received a letter from his mother about the preparations, which were not going smoothly. Some 'bright spark' had proposed that it be a male-only funeral. This had been a particularly inappropriate suggestion given that ten out of Mary's twelve offspring were actually women. Much tension had followed, and was further exacerbated by an argument about money. Olive was angry but resolute. She had never allowed herself to be pushed around and was hardly about to begin now. The matter was finally resolved and Olive was able to say her goodbyes to her mother, before returning her attention to her beloved Joe.

The following month brought searing hot temperatures and Joe's twenty-second birthday. The weather was to go down on record as one of the hottest summers of all time, permeating the ward's usual coolness with uncomfortable heat. Temperatures reached 111 degrees inside the hospital and the patients that were able to retreat to the balconies for respite did so. Joe wondered at his ability to feel comfort in the heat that others were finding unbearable. He felt warm and at ease even on the hottest of days; perhaps his time in Singapore was a contributing factor, or maybe his body was just reacting in a strange way to his treatment. It really did not matter, he enjoyed gloating as the nurses sweated.

He celebrated his birthday quietly and without visitors at Westminster Hospital. Free entertainment, unexpectedly performed beneath the ward's balcony, stemmed the boredom for a few hours, as Ray Milland and Burgess Meredith filmed scenes for a new movie as the patients looked on from above. The takes and retakes fascinated Joe, especially since both actors were in stuffy raincoats and running up and down the fire escape in the tortuous heat of the day.

Mac's former 'skipper' and friend, Harry Warwick, peppered the days with visits. Even Harry's mother came to see Mac in hospital, feeling the shared loyalty between the two former comrades. Harry brought Mac to his home for a day visit, and introduced him to his new baby daughter, Jenny. Mac was deeply touched by the continued friendship of this man who he had so admired and respected as a leader.

The letters from Joseph to Olive began to dry up as the weeks went on. Joe was struggling, and parts of his body were beginning to complain in ways he had never experienced before. He constantly had backache, and indigestion was a recurring problem. A glandular reaction to the X-ray treatment had now caused a large and conspicuous swelling in his neck, which was subsequently treated with more X-ray therapy. Most of the time, he felt tired and grim and unable to muster the energy to write letters in his now spidery scrawl.

His continued persistence that Olive should use her Sundays to rest her legs, and save her money for better use than he could put it to, made Olive's heart lurch. What pride she felt in her son's selfless attitude, at a time when he was entitled to some indulgence and self-pity. She was not 'buying' any of it, however. She could see with her own eyes and from the deterioration of his writing that Joseph was in trouble. He was a shadow of the boy she had seen before he left for Singapore and she feared the worst, while not daring to say it aloud.

She continued to send Joe news from home, hoping that the stories of normal family life would encourage him. God knows, she wanted time to stand still. It was hard to pursue the daily grind, but what choice did she have? The normality of the family routine, and the reliance of her three younger children upon her financially and emotionally, forced her onwards, one day at a time.

The summer came, although it lifted no one's spirits in the way it normally would. Joyce and Brian both sat their end-of-year exams and Olive watched them study. Dennis took to the school field, as usual, for Sports Day, and Olive celebrated his victories. The washing was washed, the pies got baked, and life went on.

Joe was truthful about his illness, but his assertions that he was OK continued, partly out of belief that he would recover, but mostly out of a natural desire to fool his mother into not worrying about rushing to his side.

On Thursday 4 September 1947, Olive received a letter from her son, which she had no idea would become so significant. The envelope is marked in Olive's desperate, spindly handwriting with the words 'Last Letter', which were added later. Olive and the children visited Joe for what would be, unknown to them, the final time, three days later.

Joseph Henry Thompson lost his battle with cancer on 22 September 1947. He was twenty-two years old. Mac never got to marry his beloved Jean. His funeral took place in Birmingham four days later, when he finally made it home for the end of his journey. He is mourned still.

Westminster Hosp.

Thursday. 4th

Dear Mom & All,

Being as it is late I'm afraid this will be but a short letter. The paper & envelopes are all "My favourite Nurse" could get and the pen is Jocks, in the next bed. I recieved your letter last week o.k. and today had one from Joyce bless her! Hope you will understand how awkward it is for me to write.

Don't worry about me
I'm no worse but
this rotten "never the
same spot twice" ache
gets me down lots of
the time during the
day so much so that
I'm far from literary in
mind or really
energetic in body.
I've finished that last
course of X ray; it was
only short as you
can see and has had
the desired effect
apparantly. What
happenes now I don't
know but Stanford Cade

is back from holiday now so when he's seen me things should start moving. They generally do!! I just hope you get this by Saturday as I want to "threaten" you now not to bring half of the family rations and tastiest bits for me. Of course I appreciate them, but you could appreciate 'em just as well if not better than me at home. See!!!

So now you know Aline
came lightly laden
on Sunday. I get more
out of seeing you or
the mob than grub.
Harry & Joan came to
see me on Sunday
and yet again; Harry
mother came on Wednes
-day afternoon. It's really
very kind of them &
I do so appreciate
their visits and the
stuff they bring.
I'm luckier than many
and don't fully realise
it! Well this is all
for now Aline so

I will close up for now. See you Sunday luv

lots of love

+ + + + +
+ + + +
+ +

P.S. Please excuse awfull writing but can't get any place flat for pad!

x x x

Epilogue

Mac's journey may have begun in 1943, a quarter of a century before I was even born, but my entrance into his life did not commence until 2010 upon the discovery of the shoe box crammed with Joe's faded handwritten envelopes.

Once it had become apparent that my dad had been equally in the dark about these letters, our joint quest to research and explore them became doubly important to both of us. Joe had passed away just days before my father's thirteenth birthday. He had lost his father, his grandmother, and his oldest sibling within a very short period of his young life and he had clearly parcelled up his pain and filed it away deeply within his memory, afraid to open it up again. After Olive died in 1978 at the age of eighty, Joyce, who had never married, but lived with and cared for her mother in her later years, inherited the correspondence, among Olive's other possessions.

The grief that my dad had buried as a child bubbled back to the surface, and as a seventy-five-year-old man, he was now able to read the true experiences of his long-dead sibling in his own words. I shall eternally be grateful that my father had this opportunity to process his grief and to put to rest any demons that may have existed before the letters came into our lives.

Once our research was completed, there was one final thing to do. Aided by information from the Commonwealth War Graves Commission and with my family in tow, I sought out Joseph's military grave at St Laurence church in Northfield, Birmingham. As I took a photograph of the headstone, I said a few words, so that my children might understand the importance of this man we had never even met. I was conscious of the lump in my throat as I spoke, and the culmination of my research, my resulting pseudo-closeness to Joe, and the presence of my own tall teenage son beside me. I had regularly, unintentionally, but inevitably, found myself firmly in the shoes of Olive during this process, she being a similar age to myself at the time of Joe's death, and it was impossible not to empathise with this woman who loved and raised her children in the most difficult of circumstances, only to lose her firstborn so cruelly and tragically.

Bill Perry: Bomb Aimer

In 2012, I decided to make an attempt to trace Mac's former crew and associates from 218 Squadron. My first clue came with online news cuttings and the rather grim discovery that Bomb Aimer Bill Perry had also met such a tragic end. I was shocked, however, when I learned that he had actually passed away even earlier than Mac. Bill, as described, had died at the height of the crew's active operations in a freak accident on the way back to Chedburgh in February 1945 at just twenty-one years old. Investigations led me to newspaper articles and I was further horrified to read that Bill's parents had lost another of their three sons to the war already. There is no mention of Bill's death in any of Joe's surviving letters, although he was almost certainly present at the funeral with the rest of the crew, as Bill was highly regarded by Mac and his other crew members as a bomb aimer and a friend.

This was not good news. I was pessimistic about my chances of finding any of the other crew members alive.

Harry Warwick: Skipper, 131051

A letter to the lovely Margery Griffiths from the 218 Squadron Association gave me a glimmer of hope, however. She personally remembered Harry Warwick and the crew, having spent her war years as a WAAF driving trucks around the Chedburgh airbase. She knew that Harry had sadly passed away, but that it had been in recent years (a very happy thought for me that he had lived a long and fruitful life after the war). She found a very old correspondence address, and it was with a great deal of trepidation that I drafted a speculative letter to Harry's widow, Joan. What do you say to a complete stranger when enquiring about their deceased husband? Enclosing photos of the crew to prove my authenticity and explaining that I was eager to research their story, I posted the letter with a little kiss for luck.

A few weeks later, having assumed that I had reached another dead end, I received an email from a lovely lady named Jenny Burton. She advised me—to my shock and excitement—that she was in fact Harry Warwick's only daughter. The Jenny whom Mac had met as a new-born baby so long ago. Her mother, now in her nineties, was still very much alive, and they were, thankfully, thrilled to hear from me. This was a major breakthrough and a huge relief.

As the weeks and months progressed, Jenny and I corresponded by email, sharing photographs, anecdotes, and emotions. Our contact had prompted Jenny to look over her father's belongings, which had been untouched for a long period of time, among which she had discovered a small box. Its contents were very moving. In this small box, Harry had secreted a number of token items relating to each of his deceased former crew members. He had always kept them secure and close, in honour of each of them. Among these items was an envelope that contained a letter to Harry, written in Joe's shaky handwriting from his hospital bed. It was dated July 1947, just two months before he passed away. In it he describes Jenny's birth and a happy visit with Harry, Joan, and the new baby while in hospital. The letter was folded around a black-rimmed card, which Harry had retained as a memento from Joe's funeral. Jenny kindly insisted that it be returned to its 'rightful resting place' within the Thompson family and it is now in my possession. For this we shall be eternally grateful.

I have since come to learn a little more about Harry and his story. He was born into a Westminster family but his father had tragically died from the flu epidemic after the First World War. Harry was raised by his mother and followed in his father's footsteps, becoming a policeman. He served in the East End before the war began and his experience of the Blitz was a trigger for volunteering for flying. In August 1941, he signed up and was sent off on the *Queen Mary* troop ship to Florida to train. He spent two years in America, going on to become an instructor, which is how he came to miss the first part of the war. The benefit of this, for his soon-to-be crew, was that Harry returned a very experienced and competent pilot. It is obvious that they held him in particularly high regard, and Jenny can remember her father commenting later in life on how he 'could have "ditched" the Lancaster blindfolded' because he had practiced the manoeuvre so many times in Florida.

Harry and Joan married during the course of Joe's stories. After their first disastrous sortie, Harry, like so many other young men of Bomber Command, was very concerned that he would not survive the war and so they struck while the iron was hot, with Navigator Alec as best man.

After the war, Harry returned briefly to the police, but after the excitement of flying, he found it to be rather dull. He turned back to flying and was eventually awarded a commercial pilot's licence. The excitement continued in the form of time spent working in Iraq and Kuwait during the first oil explorations, and then in the '50s onwards with long-term stints on government contracts in British Guiana (Guyana), the West Indies, and other far-flung locations, the family joining him much of the time.

Harry eventually became Chief Pilot for Hunting Aerosurveys and ran their flying division until he retired in 1979 for a quieter life in Devon. Harry has two grandchildren, now in their thirties, and they have a wealth of incredible stories to pass on. He was awarded the DFC in November 1945.

Ivor Turley: Tail-End Charlie

It took me several continents and a good deal of detective work to find the family of the man who, it later transpired, came from just a few miles away from Joe's own home.

My contact with the 218 Squadron Association had provided me with a highly treasured abbreviated account of the crew's 'ditching', which has been used to provide some of the detail of the same incident in this book. It had been written by Ivor Turley, and I was told that it had been donated by his family in New Zealand when they had discovered it, shortly after he had passed away in the 1990s.

This was another blow. I was, of course, hoping against all hope that I might find members of the crew still alive. Call me an optimist if you will. The account of the ditching incident turned out to have been submitted by Ivor's son-in-law, so I set about attempting to trace him online via an old email address. An online search eventually led me to a helpful HR department in South Africa—the former employers of the man I sought—who agreed to forward my emails to him. A little patience and a lot of good luck finally brought a wonderful set of email correspondence with the oldest son of Ivor Turley, Chris.

Like Jenny, Chris has been an enormous assistance in this process. He has willingly shared photographs and personal information about his father, which have helped me to form a holistic view of the man and fellow gunner whom my uncle called his friend and with whom he spent so many hours, under the best and worst of circumstances.

Ivor was the crew's rear gunner. The 'Tail-End Charlie' to Mac's mid-upper. They had an enormous amount in common. Despite the obvious gunnery discipline and being assigned to consecutive ITWs (Initial Training Wing—Joe 15, Ivor 14, both stationed at Bridlington), as far as it is possible to tell, Mac and Ivor did not actually meet until they 'crewed up' together in June 1944 at Upper Heyford. During the course of conversations with Chris Turley, it also became apparent that both men hailed from Birmingham, a fact that had been unknown to me before making contact with Chris. They volunteered via the same recruitment centre and were even assigned sequential service numbers. We have both found ourselves wondering whether they may have even stood beside each other in that queue in 1943. We shall never know, but the coincidence is undeniable.

Alec Stott: Navigator 162273

Alexander Haldane Stott was the crew's navigator. Although I have, at the time of writing, been unable to trace any of Alec's family, I have discovered that he remained in the RAF after the war, eventually rising to the heady status of squadron leader. In 1960, as a squadron leader, he was recognised by the Queen in her birthday honours list and was awarded the MBE.

Just two years later, tragedy struck when, on 16 November 1962, Alec was involved in a high profile, fatal helicopter crash at sea. He was thirty-eight years old and sadly died in the accident. Alec had been one of three passengers and the helicopter had been transporting the VIPs from HMS *Hermes* back to the mainland, off the coast of south Wales. Engine failure had resulted in the disaster, which also took the life of member of the House of Lords, Lord Windlesham. The accident was mentioned in the House of Lords just a few days after it had taken place, and the following is an extract from the statement made on the subject by Lord Carrington, First Lord of the Admiralty at that time:

> My Lords, the helicopter belonging to HMS *Hermes* was carrying three passengers—Lord Windlesham, Mr Cronin, the Member of Parliament for Loughborough, and an RAF officer, Squadron Leader Stott—from the ship to the RN Air Station, Brawdy. Lord Windlesham and Mr Cronin had been spending a period at sea in HMS *Hermes* under an Admiralty scheme to enable Members of both Houses of Parliament to visit the Fleet. One mile west of South Bishop's Island, while flying at a height of 1,000 feet, the aircraft suffered a total engine failure and came down in the sea. It came down slowly under auto-rotation but on striking the rough water, it immediately rolled over, submerging the door. It sank in less than a minute.
>
> Mr Cronin and the crew of two were rescued alive and unhurt by another helicopter from HMS *Hermes*, after being in the water for about half an hour. Squadron Leader Stott was also picked up unconscious, but I am sorry to say that he subsequently died. Lord Windlesham was not picked up, and I very much regret that, in spite of a prolonged search of the area by aircraft from HMS *Hermes* and from the RN Air Station, Brawdy, in which HM Ships *Duchess*, *Berwick*, *Scarborough*, and *Lowestoft*, as well as the St David's lifeboat, took part, no trace of him has been found. On behalf of the Admiralty and the Royal Navy, I desire to express my profound regret at this tragic accident and my deep sympathy to Lady Windlesham and to Mrs Stott.
>
> A Board of Inquiry assembled yesterday on-board HMS *Hermes*. Its report is expected in a few days. An attempt is being made to salvage the helicopter which is lying in 26 fathoms.

Alec, who had been Harry's best man at his wedding in 1945, was certainly very much missed.

'Smokey' Joe Lee: Fellow Trainee Gunner

The cheerful Scouser and fellow 'Joe' turned out to be every inch the cheeky chap I had imagined when we finally came face to face with each other in June 2014. Extensive research into the potential whereabouts of Mac's former best friend, Joe Lee, one of the six original 'Joes' from the ACRC, eventually led me to an address on The Wirral. This time, fortune was in my favour when Joe's granddaughter, Mandy, replied to my correspondence confirming, to my absolute thrill, that Joe was alive and well and, most importantly, as excited as I was at the prospect of finally reuniting our two families.

With an enormous debt of gratitude to Project Propeller, the wonderful annual reunion organisation for former Second World War aircrew, private air transport was provided for myself, Joe, and his daughter and granddaughter, and we met with a teary embrace on a hot sunny day in a field beside Gloucester airport.

Joe happily passed on his stories about his long-lost friend and was keen that I should know it was he who had facilitated Mac's first meeting with Jean at that fairground in Liverpool back in 1944. It was, he told me, Jean who had knocked on the front door of his home in September 1947 to break the dreadful news that her fiancé was dead. It was a moment he had not forgotten.

Joe wrote me a wonderful letter in 2014, which I treasure. He told me all that had happened to him since Mac's story ended, including marrying the lovely Dot in 1947 and the three children and wonderful life they had together before she passed away in 2002. Following his posting to the OTU at Silverstone, he had joined 50 Squadron at Skellingthorpe near Lincoln, completing eleven operations. A stint in the Far East followed, before he was demobbed in 1946. Joe then went back to his former trade for a while as a joiner, but later found a career as a police officer on Merseyside, where he served for thirty years.

In 1963, a chance incident put every bit of Joe's military and police training to good use when he and two other police officers heard the cries of a man who had fallen into the Mersey river. Joe immediately lowered himself into the water with a rope tied under his armpits and proceeded to bring the man, who was clinging for dear life to a pontoon, to safety. The man, who was unable to swim, had been swept by the ebbing tide from the Seacombe ferry landing stage and was dragged beneath a second landing stage, where he had managed to grab hold of something and scream for help. Joe, with the help of his colleague, managed to pull the man to safety. His brave actions earned him the British Empire Medal for Gallantry.

In the short time I knew Smokey Joe—who incidentally, like Mac, never really understood where the 'Smokey' bit came from—I could see exactly what had drawn my uncle to him. He exuded warmth and fun and it was with a very heavy heart that I learned of his subsequent death in 2014 from his granddaughter. He told me that he considered it an honour to have known Mac; I can only say that the feeling is entirely mutual.

Jean

Here, possibly, lies the greatest story of them all. Enquiries with my aunt, whose memory was, by her own admission, a little faded after almost seventy years, recalled that Jean had found further happiness and had gone on to marry a few years after the loss of Joe. She and her family had stayed in touch with our own for a significant period of time, even visiting and sending Christmas cards for some years. Eventually, as time went on, the contact understandably dwindled. Jean had remained in her home town of Liverpool, where she was very happy, very loved, and had raised her own family.

My feelings about potentially contacting Jean were confused. It was likely to prove impossible to find her anyway, and even if I did, how might she or her family feel about the intrusion of a complete stranger who wanted to talk about her former fiancée? I was worried that this would be, at best, a delicate subject.

My research began with a search of the Liverpool marriages and deaths registers. I had no idea who Jean had married, but had to assume that it was within a certain time period. This information led to one or two possible contacts and with them came the sad realisation that Jean may well have passed away in recent years. Armed with an address for Jean's potential next of kin, I took the plunge and wrote the most difficult but tactful letter of my life.

When my phone rang days later, I almost fell off my chair. A lovely lady with a rich Liverpool accent declared herself to be Ann, the youngest daughter of Jean. It was overwhelming and a huge relief to hear Ann say that she was delighted to hear from me. Her mother had indeed, sadly, passed away, but she had always been open about her near-marriage to Joe, and both her husband and children had known about his existence, although understandably, they had little information about his full story.

We chatted and emailed and she put me in contact with Mary, Jean's younger sister, who, along with Joan Warwick and Joe Lee, are the only surviving contemporaries of Joe's that I have found so far. Mary, I am told, to this day still wears the engagement ring that Joe gave to Jean all those years ago. A thought that still makes me gush with emotion.

Out of respect for the privacy of Jean's family, I have chosen not to reveal their full names in this book.

My research into Joe's story and crew is still a work-in-progress. I have, to date, been unsuccessful in tracing the whereabouts, families, or further stories of Tom Waring, Joe Naisbitt, Bill Perry, or Alec Stott.

I set out to perform a simple task: to record the adventures of a very young man with a fascinating, but ultimately tragic story through his letters home. It has turned out to be so much more than just a pile of letters, becoming an adventure of my own, which I can pass over to my children and theirs; a critical episode in the history of my family, and of our country.

It is with the deepest regret that I am unable to share this final document with my father, Brian, who we sadly lost in September 2014, before it turned into a book. Shortly after his death, my family and I adopted two children. Our new son has proudly taken Joseph as his new middle name.

To lose a twenty-two-year-old son would profoundly affect any parent for the rest of his or her life. For Olive, the endurance of a husband-less war was made bearable only by the mature and loving relationship that she held with her eldest son. He stepped into the role of provider and their mutual affection and support for each other sustained the family through years of difficulties. His untimely and cruel loss profoundly affected his mother and siblings for the rest of their lives and he is mourned still.

It is to Olive's enormous credit that Mac, albeit for just a brief period, proved himself to be one of the very finest of the young men of Bomber Command.

It is to my shame that it took me over forty years to recognise that the young man in the never-mentioned portrait was our family hero. It is, however, now also my privilege to be able to finally make right that wrong and to capture in this book the story of the man I never met, who has changed my life.